GANG POLITICS

Revolution, Repression, and Crime

Kristian Williams

Foreword by Robert Evans

Gang Politics: Revolution, Repression, and Crime
© 2022 Kristian Williams
This edition © 2022 AK Press
ISBN: 978-1-84935-456-1
E-ISBN: 978-1-84935-457-8
Library of Congress Control Number: 2021944670

AK Press
370 Ryan Ave. #100
Chico, CA 95973
www.akpress.org
akpress@akpress.org

AK Press
33 Tower St.
Edinburgh EH6 7BN
Scotland
www.akuk.com
akuk@akpress.org

The above addresses would be delighted to provide you with the latest AK Press
distribution catalog, which features books, pamphlets, zines, and stylish apparel
published and/or distributed by AK Press. Alternatively, visit our websites for the
complete catalog, latest news, and secure ordering.

Cover design by Tim Simons: www.tlsimons.com
Printed in Canada on acid-free paper

CONTENTS

Street Fights and Revolution in the City of Roses

Robert Evans

For almost three years now, I've reported on the running street battles between Portland-area antifascists, the Proud Boys, and police.
In that time I've watched the city's antifascist movement shrink,
from a broad popular coalition to a smaller, hardened core of activists. This is less reflective of antifascism's popularity in the City
of Roses than it is of the danger of confronting the far right in the
streets. Gunfire is now very close to guaranteed at any sizable confrontation.

As Kristian Williams ably traces, the Proud Boys got their start
as a gang. As we enter the Biden years, they might seem on the
edge of morphing into an insurgency. This impression is deceptive,
though. The Proud Boys have not gone out of their way to win the
hearts and minds of the public. Instead, they've supplicated themselves to the levers of power. They've volunteered their time and
efforts to act as an armed wing of the Republican Party and an
auxiliary to the local police. The police in the Pacific Northwest
have responded by allowing the Proud Boys and their affiliates to
run wild, without interference, so long as their targets are anyone
vaguely on "the left."

Gangs and states very much exist on the same continuum, and
the conflicts between them largely arise from the ability of gangs
to challenge the state's monopoly on power. What we've seen
with the Proud Boys is that many agents of the state are willing to

approve the "legitimate" use of violence as long as these foot soldiers for fascism do not fundamentally challenge their benefactors. As Covid-19 precautions are increasingly politicized, Proud Boys have been allowed to accost school board meetings and threaten schools themselves in the name of "medical freedom."

It was not until I read Kristian's work that I started to think about the Proud Boys and what they represent in a much more functional manner. At the end of the day, these far-right groups aren't just showing up to fight for the hell of it; they're presenting a very specific audience with an alternative view of what the state could be. The widespread refusal of American law enforcement to act against the Proud Boys suggests that this audience has liked what they've seen.

On the other side of things, antifascists have come to increasingly resemble an insurgency. The growth of mutual aid networks accelerated in 2020 thanks to the pressures of the coronavirus and the BLM protests. This has led to a situation J. Edgar Hoover would have abhorred, and it has at times provided anarchism in particular with the best popular PR in modern U.S. history.

But I have seen uglier things develop on the left as well. Kristian notes that Anti-Racist Action and the SHARPs started life as a gang, which turned toward the cause of racial justice. In some places, particularly Portland, I see a risk that organized antifascism will evolve away from this and shift more into the shape of a gang. I've seen elements of this on the ground in Portland: small groups declaring themselves "security" and using force—paintball guns and mace—on neighbors or fellow protesters who break "the rules."

Whoever fights monsters should see to it that, in the process, they do not become a monster. The same is true with fighting a gang like the Proud Boys. In the past year, I have watched as paintball and airsoft guns, as well as the indiscriminate deployment of bear mace, have gone from staples of far-right street fighters to ubiquitous on both sides. The appeal is obvious; when you're shot with a paintball, it's natural to want to shoot back.

But I think yielding to the far right in this way is its own sort of defeat. There are times when weapons must be used, but nine times out of ten a fire extinguisher loaded with paint does more damage than an airsoft rifle ever could. Rotten eggs damage gear more than paintballs. Raw force will always avail antifascists less than cleverness and surprise.

Law enforcement would, of course, love nothing more than to see decentralized, horizontal packs of affinity groups turn into something more centralized, violent, and foolish. They would much rather deal with a street gang, engaged in running gun battles and casual brutality to bystanders, than a proper insurgent force that offers a compelling alternative to the state.

In tracing the devolution of the Black Panthers and the history of the Blackstone Nation, Kristian provides rubrics for how the future of antifascism and the militant left might soon look. Today's activists would do well to pay attention to these historic examples. This is vital work, because only with such a rubric can we hope to avoid the missteps of the past.

September 2021
Portland, Oregon

Questioning under Caution

An Introductory Note

Bloods and Crips. Rangers and Panthers. Police and thieves. Proud Boys and Antifa. Insurgency and counterinsurgency. Revolution and counterrevolution. Politics and crime.

How different are these? And how are they alike?

In these three essays, written over the course of a dozen years, I explore the complex intersections between gangs and politics and argue that government and criminality are intimately related. The first essay, "The Other Side of the COIN," examines the adaptation of the strategies and techniques of counterinsurgency warfare to domestic law enforcement, with particular attention to the policing of gangs. In the second essay, "Gangs, States, and Insurgencies," I pose the next obvious question: If the police take a counterinsurgency approach to combating gangs, what does that suggest about the relationship between gangs and insurgencies and the state's attitude toward each? The third essay, "Street Fights, Gang Wars, and Insurrections," applies my analysis to two groups that are often in the headlines—the Proud Boys and Antifa—and considers the ways that they each adhere to or diverge from the idea of the politicized gang, the degree to which that mode of organizing coheres with their politics, and the very different treatment each has received from the authorities. Throughout the book, I emphasize both the potential and the limitations of the gang form for liberatory politics.

In a sense, a *gang* is an inherently political formation and set of activities, involving the concentration and application of power, thereby influencing the distribution of resources within a community. The same may be said of the police, whatever the cops themselves happen to think about it. Both are therefore political, whether or not they self-consciously adhere to an identifiable ideology. When gangs *do* adopt an explicitly political program, the results tend to be mixed. Even with a new orientation, which will sometimes bring prestige and other benefits, they will nevertheless likely retain, and be constrained by, the gang's established structure, culture, and strategy. Ultimately, an organization's form may matter as much as the intentions of even its most powerful leaders.

As I researched these questions, and especially as I saw their increasing relevance for contemporary events, my thinking on gangs changed considerably. I have edited the earlier writing to reflect the ways that my ideas have developed, but astute readers may yet notice some shifts in tone, changes in perspective, and subtle differences in terminology between one essay and the next. To some degree that is an inevitable, if unfortunate, result of repurposing material more than a decade after it was produced. But there is also an element of ambiguity and approximation inherent to the subject.

Resisting Definition

What it is that makes a group a gang is always contested, and the gang form itself may be more fluid than taxonomists would prefer.

The *Penguin Dictionary of Sociology* offers under "gang": "this term is typically used to refer to small groups which are bound together by a common sense of loyalty and territory, and which are hierarchically structured around a gang leader."[1] The more current and technical "Eurogang" definition, popular among criminologists, describes a gang as "any durable, street-oriented youth group whose own identity includes involvement in illegal activity."[2] The U.S. Department of Justice provides this definition:

Gangs are associations of three or more individuals who adopt a group identity in order to create an atmosphere of fear or intimidation. Gangs are typically organized upon racial, ethnic, or political lines and employ common names, slogans, aliases, symbols, tattoos, style of clothing, hairstyles, hand signs or graffiti. The association's primary purpose is to engage in criminal activity and the use of violence or intimidation to further its criminal objectives and enhance or preserve the association's power, reputation, or economic resources. Gangs are also organized to provide common defense of its members and interests from rival criminal organizations or to exercise control over a particular location or region.[3]

In each case, criminologists try to encode in the definition conclusions about what I think must be (and remain) empirical questions concerning features like the gang's size, methods, purpose, affective ties, territoriality, structure, longevity, urbanity, demographics, public presentation, and self-conception. I find that on this narrow issue the commonsense meaning and even the pop-culture stereotypes may have more going for them than the criminological definitions. If you consider what the gangs have in common in such varied films as *The Gangs of New York*, *Boyz n the Hood*, *The Warriors*, and even *West Side Story*, I think you would have a pretty good idea of what people mean to invoke when they use the word *gang*.[4]

Equally troublesome is the concept of *crime*. In legal terms, of course, crime just refers to that body of illegal activity that can be prosecuted in the criminal courts (as opposed to being regulated by an administrative body, for example). But the term also carries a kind of moral implication, such that violations of certain fundamental norms—kidnapping, extortion, or murder, for example— may be coherently thought of as criminal, even when permitted by law and authorized by the state. Here there are two commonsense meanings, with a great deal of overlap but some important distinctions. The essence of *crime* remains uncertain.[5]

As I hope to make clear throughout this slim volume, I consider this sort of indeterminacy to be an advantage. The blurring of these lines, the complication of our categories, is among my purposes in writing.

Labels and Frames

The authorities, especially the police, like to describe certain militant groups as "gangs" for a variety of reasons, some technical and some political.

Most simply, a *gang* is a type of organization with which they are already familiar. The label brings with it an interpretative frame, a way of understanding the phenomenon. It allows the authorities to fit the new organization into their existing categories and procedures. They *already have* gang squads, gang files, and a range of laws and strategies designed for countering gangs. Labeling a group a gang is thus as much a matter of selecting the right tools for countering it as it is one of understanding the organization itself. Such ready-made templates, of course, risk oversimplification and error, but such may yet be preferable to confronting a novel, unfamiliar, and (for the moment) incomprehensible adversary.

Then again, sometimes oversimplification is precisely the point. There is a propaganda value to calling your opponents a gang. The term itself, in respectable circles, is assumed to be both depoliticizing and delegitimizing. It denies the value or validity of any cause the organization may espouse, and it frames the countervailing police action as normal law enforcement rather than political repression. Naturally, as both *crime* and *gangs* are commonly conceptualized in racial terms (that is, racist terms), some groups are more likely to receive the *gang* label than others, and those groups operating among populations that are already over-policed and presumptively criminalized are the most likely of all.

Interestingly, however, the gang frame can also justify police *inaction,* or even indifference—especially in the case of rightwing gangs. Discounting the politics means that the authorities can ignore racist graffiti, meetings, and rallies, rather than seeing them as part of a campaign of intimidation. Even actual violence, provided that it is directed against another "gang"—that is, against another opponent of the state—may receive minimal attention, being cynically treated as a case of one problem solving another. And, by viewing both leftwing and rightwing militants as gangs, the police can treat them as equivalent, in effect downplaying the violence of the right while exaggerating the violence of the left.

Naturally, my interest in investigating gangs is entirely different from, and at many points directly opposed to, the cops' interest in doing so. And nothing I say in this volume should be taken as justifying the childish notion that calling a group of people a "gang" automatically makes them the bad guys, or that designating one gang "the police" somehow makes them the good guys.

Questions and Interpretations

What is interesting to me is not whether the various groups I discuss here *are* gangs in some definitive sense, but whether they may be *understood as gangs*, whether or not they understand themselves that way, and what features and dynamics become apparent under that interpretation.

I hope that this discussion may help inform our thinking not merely about gangs but also about a wider range of questions related to conflict, repression, legitimacy, and the state. Those questions are basic to any radical organizing, and our answers—or, more often, our unexamined assumptions—may determine a whole range of subsequent choices about the types of organizations we build, the basis of our solidarity, our political strategy, our tactical preferences, and the cultural expression of our values. The stakes here are sometimes absurdly high, and they are often more real than we allow ourselves to recognize. If nothing else, I believe the stories I tell in these essays underscore the need to take care how we organize, especially if part of what we are organizing is the capacity for violence.

The Other Side of the Coin

Counterinsurgency and Community Policing

Prologue: Saving America

In August 2011, British prime minister David Cameron called William Bratton to ask his advice concerning the riots sweeping the United Kingdom following a police shooting.

That is a curious and revealing fact, especially since Bratton's reputation—as police chief in New York City, then in Los Angeles—was not built on his handling of riots or his response to controversies over police violence. He is known, instead, for declaring war on panhandlers and gangs. Given Bratton's heavy-handed, "zero-tolerance" approach and tough-guy reputation, his advice was also notable: "Community policing is the philosophy that saved America in the 1990s," he told the BBC. "It's about partnership, the police working with the community."[1]

To understand what these things have to do with one another—riots, gangs, "zero tolerance," and "community policing"—it is important to understand the nature of counterinsurgency warfare. This essay argues that, despite the term's association with colonialism and Latin American "dirty wars," many contemporary counterinsurgency practices were developed by police agencies inside the United States and continue to be used against the domestic population.

Part One: Repression, Counterinsurgency, and the State

Ends and Means: Legitimacy and Statecraft

Counterinsurgency—COIN in the military jargon—is not simply synonymous with *repression* but has a narrow, technical meaning, which relies on the definition of *insurgency*. U.S. Army Field Manual 3-24, *Counterinsurgency*, explains: "[An] insurgency [is] an organized movement aimed at the overthrow of a constituted government through the use of subversion and armed conflict . . . . Stated another way, an insurgency is an organized, protracted politico-military struggle designed to weaken the control and legitimacy of an established government, occupying power, or other political authority while increasing insurgent control." The definition of *counterinsurgency* logically follows: "Counterinsurgency is military, paramilitary, political, economic, psychological, and civic actions taken by a government to defeat insurgency."[2]

Counterinsurgency, then, refers to both a type of war and a style of warfare. The term describes a kind of military operation outside of conventional army-versus-army war-fighting and is sometimes called "low-intensity" or "asymmetrical" combat. But *counter-insurgency* also describes a particular perspective on how such operations ought to be managed. This style of warfare is characterized by an emphasis on intelligence, security and peacekeeping operations, population control, propaganda, and efforts to gain the trust of the people.

This last point is the crucial one. As FM 3-24 declares: *"Legitimacy is the main objective."*[3]

The primary aim of counterinsurgency is political.[4] That's why, in the context of the U.S. occupation of Iraq, we heard career officers arguing that "victory in combat is only a penultimate step in the larger task of 'winning the peace.'"[5] And it's the need for legitimacy that they were referring to when they said: "Military action is necessary . . . but it is not sufficient. There needs to be a political aspect."[6]

The political ends rely in large part on political means. As the RAND Corporation's David Gompert and John Gordon explain: "In COIN, the outcomes are decided mainly in the human dimension, by the contested population, and the capabilities of opposing armed forces are only one factor in determining those outcomes. The people will decide whether the state or the insurgents offer a better future, and to a large extent which of the two will be given the chance."[7] The RAND report is titled, appropriately, *War by Other Means*. War, as Clausewitz observed, is politics by other means; and politics, as Foucault reasoned, is war by other means.[8] But in counterinsurgency, the means are not so "other." In COIN, war-fighting is characterized by the same elements as state-building—establishing legitimacy, controlling territory, and monopolizing violence.[9]

What sets COIN apart from other theories of repression, I believe, is the self-conscious acknowledgement that the state *needs* legitimacy to stabilize its rule, and that under conditions of insurgency its legitimacy is slipping. In other words, from the perspective of counterinsurgency, resistance is not simply a matter of the population (or portions of it) refusing to cooperate with the state's agenda; resistance comes as a consequence of the state failing to meet the needs of the population.

It is possible, therefore, to see COIN as representing "liberal" or even "radical" politics.[10] Yet such apologetics miss the larger point. As a matter of realpolitik, the authorities have to respond in some manner to popular demands; however, COIN allows them to do so in a way that at preserves their overall control and in the best case amplifies it. The purpose of counterinsurgency is to prevent any real shift in power.

Counterinsurgency is all about reclaiming the state's authority. Violence and territory are inherent to the project, but it is really legitimacy—"the consent of the governed," "societal support"— that separates the winners from the losers.[11] As Gompert and Gordon put it: "The key in COIN is not to monopolize force but to monopolize *legitimate* force."[12]

The strictly military aspects of the counterinsurgency campaign are, of course, necessary; but so are the softer, subtler efforts to bolster public support for the government. Both types of activities have to be understood as elements of political power.

The Social Science of Repression

To meet the challenges of counterinsurgency—first in restless colonies, then domestically—the security forces have had to shift their understanding of intelligence. Since the cause of an insurgency is not just a subversive conspiracy but necessarily connects to the broader features of society, the state's agents cannot simply ferret out the active cadre but need to aim at an understanding of the overall social system. The U.S. Army's counterinsurgency field manual (FM 3-24) incorporates this perspective, arguing that strategists "require insight into cultures, perceptions, values, beliefs, interests and decision-making processes of individuals and groups."[13]

This sort of intelligence work is concerned with questions that are primarily sociological.[14] And so a great deal of FM 3-24 is concerned with explicating basic social science terms like *group*, *coercive force*, and *social capital*. In fact, the entirety its Appendix B is devoted to explaining "Social Network Analysis and Other Analytic Tools." It specifies, "A social network is not just a description of who is in the insurgent organization; it is a picture of the population, how it is put together and how members interact with one another."[15] FM 3-24 specifically suggests "analyzing historical documents and records, interviewing individuals, and studying photos and books" in order to "draw an accurate picture of a network" by identifying "bonds formed over time by family, friendship, or organizational association."[16]

As one RAND Corporation report explains, counterinsurgency requires that the security forces collect both "information on specific individuals" and "information in which the actions or opinions of thousands, perhaps even millions, of people are highlighted."[17]

This broader approach changes the type of information the type of information the authorities need and also the means they use to collect it. The same report emphasizes: "Even during a security operation, the information needed for counterinsurgency is as much or more about context, population, and perceptions as it is about the hostile force . . . . [O]nly a small fraction of the information needed would likely be secret information gathered by secret means from secret sources"[18]

Properly analyzed, the RAND researchers tell us, the information the state collects can be used in five types of activity: (1) police and military operations "such as sweeps, roadblocks, or arrests"; (2) assessments of progress in the counterinsurgency campaign ("how many people have been hurt or killed in the war; what kind of crimes are being committed; who is getting employment and where; and who is staying put or leaving the country"); (3) "the provision of public services, whether security and safety services (e.g., an efficient 911 system) or social services (e.g., health care, education, and public assistance)"; (4) identifying insurgents ("[to] distinguish those willing to help from those eager to hurt"); and, (5) the coercion of individuals for purposes of winning cooperation and recruiting informants ("information about individuals may be necessary to persuade each one to help the government rather than helping the insurgents").

This last point shows something of the recursive relationship between intelligence and coercion. In an insurgency, both sides rely on the cooperation of the populace; therefore they compete for it, in part through coercive means. As RAND researcher Martin Libicki writes: "Those uncommitted to either side should weigh the possibility that the act of informing or even interacting with one side may bring down the wrath of the other side." Whoever is best able to make good on this threat, Libicki argues, will receive the best information: "The balance of coercion dictates the balance of intelligence."[19]

Part Two: Military/Policing Exchanges

A Paradigm for Pacification

In my book *Our Enemies in Blue*, one chapter, "Your Friendly Neighborhood Police State," is devoted to the argument that the two major developments in American policing since the 1960s—militarization and community policing—are actually two aspects of a domestic counterinsurgency program. I summed up the idea with a simple equation: "Community Policing + Militarization = Counterinsurgency."[20]

In the years since then, the counterinsurgency literature has made this point explicit. For example, the RAND Corporation's report *War by Other Means* lists, among the law enforcement "capabilities . . . considered to be high priority" in COIN: "well-trained and well-led community police and quick-response, light-combat-capable (constabulary) police."[21] Similarly, a Joint Special Operations University report, *Policing and Law Enforcement in COIN: The Thick Blue Line*, purports: "The predominant ways of utilizing police and law enforcement within a COIN strategy . . . consist of the adoption of the community-policing approach supported by offensive policing actions such as paramilitary operations, counterguerrilla patrolling, pseudo operations [in which state forces pose as insurgent groups], and raids."[22]

The advantages the state receives from each aspect are fairly clear. Militarization increases available force, but, as importantly, it also provides increased discipline and command and control. It reorders the police agency to allow for better coordination and teamwork, while also opening space for local initiative and officer discretion.

Community policing, meanwhile, helps to legitimize police efforts by presenting cops as problem-solvers. It forms police-driven partnerships that put additional resources at their disposal and win the cooperation of community leaders. And, by increasing daily, friendly contacts with people in the neighborhood, community policing provides a direct supply of low-level information.[23] These are not incidental features of community policing; these aspects speak to its real purpose.

In fact, one RAND Corporation study goes so far as to present community policing as its paradigm for counterinsurgency:

> Pacification is best thought of as a massively enhanced version of the "community policing" technique that emerged in the 1970s . . . . Community policing is centered on a broad concept of problem solving by law enforcement officers working in an area that is well-defined and limited in scale, with sensitivity to geographic, ethnic, and other boundaries. Patrol officers form a bond of trust with local residents, who get to know them as more than a uniform. The police work with local groups, businesses, churches, and the like to address the concerns and problems of the neighborhood. Pacification is simply an expansion of this concept to include greater development and security assistance.[24]

The military's use of police theory—in particular the adoption of a "community policing" perspective—shows a cyclical exchange between the various parts of the national security apparatus.

The Cycle of Violence: Imports and Exports

Domestically, the unrest of the 1960s left the police in a difficult position. The cops' response to the social movements of the day—the civil rights and antiwar movements especially—had cost them dearly in terms of public credibility, elite support, and officer morale. Frequent and overt recourse to violence, combined with covert (often illegal) surveillance, infiltration, and disruption, had not only failed to squelch the popular movements, it had also diminished trust in law enforcement.

The police needed to reinvent themselves, and the first place they looked for models was the military. The birth of the paramilitary unit—the SWAT team—was one result.[25] A new, more restrained, crowd control strategy was another.[26] Military training, tactics, equipment, and weaponry made their way into domestic police departments—as did veterans returning from Vietnam and, more subtly, military approaches to organization, deployment, and command and control. Police strategists specifically began studying counterinsurgency and counterguerrilla warfare.[27]

At the same time, and seemingly incongruously, police were also beginning to experiment with a "softer," more friendly type of law enforcement—foot patrols, neighborhood meetings, police-sponsored youth activities, and attention to quality-of-life issues quite apart from crime. A few radical criminologists saw this for what it was—a domestic "hearts and minds" campaign. As the Center for Research on Criminal Justice pointed out in *The Iron Fist and the Velvet Glove*: "Like the similar techniques developed in the sixties to maintain the overseas empire (on which many of the new police techniques were patterned), these new police strategies represent an attempt to streamline and mystify the repressive power of the state, not to minimize it or change its direction. The forms of repression may change, but their functions remain the same."[28]

Both militarization and community policing arose at the same time, in response to the same social pressures. And, whereas the military largely neglected COIN in the period following defeat in Vietnam, the police kept practicing and developing its techniques. Decades later, facing insurgencies in Iraq and Afghanistan, the military turned to police for ideas.[29]

The lines of influence move in both directions.

Statistical Control

Among the police innovations that COIN theorists recommend for military use are the neighborhood watch, embedded video, computerized intelligence files, and statistical analysis.[30] The last pair are particularly interesting.

In *Byting Back*, Martin Libicki explains the utility of statistical analysis programs, pointing to New York's Compstat (computerized statistics) system as an example.[31] Instituted under Chief William Bratton, Compstat worked by compiling crime reports, analyzing the emerging statistics, and presenting the information on precinct-level maps, thus enabling commanders to identify high-crime areas, deploy their officers strategically, and measure the progress of their efforts. Though its effect on actual crime is debatable, Compstat certainly served as the organizational keystone for the NYPD's city-wide crackdown during the Giuliani years.[32] Since that time, other departments around the country have adopted similar systems.[33]

The Los Angeles Police Department's system was proposed by Shannon Paulson, a police sergeant and a navy intelligence reservist. It too was implemented under the leadership of William Bratton, who had since become the LAPD chief. In Los Angeles, street cops carry a checklist of sixty-five "suspicious activities"—behaviors such as taking measurements, using binoculars, drawing diagrams, making notes, or expressing extremist views. Officers are required to file reports whenever they see such things, even if no crime has been committed. The "Suspicious Activity Reports" are then routed through the nearest fusion center, the Joint Regional Intelligence Center, where they are compiled, analyzed, and shared with other agencies—including local and national law enforcement agencies, the military, and private corporations.[34]

In the following years, similar systems were implemented in cities around the country. Perhaps the most famous example was in Camden, New Jersey, whose combination of high-tech surveillance and zero-tolerance patrols led the *Atlantic* to christen it "Surveillance City."[35] Over the course of a few months in 2013, Camden installed 121 surveillance cameras, thirty-five gunfire-locating microphones, and automatic license plate readers. Data from this monitoring network was sent to four fusion centers, where it was used to map the city's drug distribution network—and the communities in which it was embedded. Patrol officers were then provided with maps pointing to possible "hot spots" and photo albums identifying potential suspects.[36]

The technological turn was no surprise. Three years earlier, Charles McKenna, the head of the state's Office of Homeland Security and Preparedness, was open about what new computer technologies might contribute to law enforcement: "We are particularly interested in computer profiling, which is much more sophisticated, and quicker, than traditional racial profiling."[37]

Mapping Muslims

The U.S. government's mapping of the American Muslim population should be viewed in this light. In 2002 and 2003, the Department of Homeland Security requested—and received—statistical data, sorted by zip code and nationality, on people who identified themselves as "Arab" in the 2000 census.[38] And in February 2003, FBI director Robert Mueller ordered all fifty-six Bureau field offices to create "demographic" profiles of their areas of operation, specifically including the number of mosques. One Justice Department official explained that the demographics would be used "to set performance goals and objectives" for anti-terror efforts and electronic surveillance.[39]

Civil liberties groups compared the program to the first steps in the internment of Japanese Americans during World War II.[40] This notion seems less than hyperbolic if we recall that, during this same period, seven hundred Middle Eastern immigrants were arrested as they complied with new registration rules. More than twelve hundred were detained without explanation or trial following the September 11, 2001, attacks, and thousands more were "interviewed" under FBI orders.[41] At the same time, the FBI has sent infiltrators into mosques throughout the country to root out—or sometimes to set up—terror cells.[42]

In 2007, the LAPD began planning its own mapping program, dressed in the rhetoric of community policing. As the *L.A. Times* reported, the "Los Angeles Police Department's counter-terrorism bureau proposed using U.S. census data and other demographic information to pinpoint various Muslim communities and then reach out to them through social service agencies."[43]

Deputy Police Chief Michael P. Downing, head of the counter-terrorism unit, explained: "While this project will lay out geographic locations of many different Muslim populations around Los Angeles, we also intend to take a deeper look at their history, demographics, language, culture, ethnic breakdown, socioeconomic status and social interactions. . . . It is also our hope to identify communities within the larger Muslim community which may be susceptible to violent ideologically based extremism and then use a full spectrum approach guided by intelligence-led strategy."[44] After widespread public outcry, the LAPD publicly repudiated the plan.

Based on the Los Angeles controversy, the New York Police Department decided to keep its surveillance secret. Developed with CIA assistance—advice, training, and embedded staff—the NYPD's program was modeled on Israeli intelligence operations in the West Bank. The department's Demographic Unit uses census data to identify Muslim neighborhoods and sends undercover officers to monitor the conversations at hookah bars, cafes, and restaurants, as well as the literature at book stores. At the same time, the Terrorism Interdiction Unit recruits informants to report on neighborhood activities and monitor the sermons delivered at mosques. When young men of Middle Eastern descent are arrested—regardless of the nature of the charge—they are commonly interrogated by intelligence officers as part of the department's "debriefing program." Muslim prisoners are promised better conditions if they provide information. And the department has used minor licensing problems or traffic violations to pressure Pakistani taxi drivers to become informants.

Based on the resultant information, police analysts have produced a report assessing every mosque in the city for its possible terrorist ties. One NYPD official justified the program using a term that originated with the House Un-American Activities

Committee (in a report on the Black Panthers) and that has since been carried forward into the counterinsurgency literature: The point, he said, is to "map the city's human terrain."[45]

Zero Tolerance in the War on Terror

None of the NYPD's spy games should have been particularly surprising. It was, with some variation, more or less in line with what some top police theorists were publicly recommending.

In 2006, the criminologist George L. Kelling and L.A. police chief William Bratton wrote an article titled "Policing Terrorism" for the Manhattan Institute's *Civic Bulletin*.[46] Kelling was one of the authors of the "broken windows" theory underlying police zero-tolerance campaigns.[47] Bratton was one of the strategy's foremost practitioners. In their article, they explain that the cops' "everyday presence" in a designated area—the basis of community policing—means that patrol officers are well-placed to "notice even subtle changes in the neighborhoods they patrol." And: "They are in a better position to know responsible leaders in the Islamic and Arabic communities and can reach out to them for information and for help in developing informants."[48] At the same time, cops can ask "business owners . . . [as well as] doormen, private security guards, and transit workers"—ultimately, the "general public"—to "remain vigilant, to report any suspicious activity to police, and to 'ask the next question'"—that is, to stay "alert to preventive and investigatory possibilities" (or, less politely, to snoop).[49]

Once collected, the information provided by these various sources can be entered into a Compstat-type system for analysis and "to share data . . . across jurisdictions and levels of government."[50] It's for these reasons that fusion centers and Joint Terrorism Task Forces (JTTFs) are important. The fusion centers "pool information from multiple jurisdictions," making it possible to share information "horizontally," while the JTTFs help it to flow "vertically," between the locals and the feds.[51]

At the same time, Kelling and Bratton advocate "creating a

hostile environment for terrorists" by focusing on "illegal border crossings, forged documents, and other relatively minor precursor crimes," by increasing police visibility to "create a sense of omnipresence," and by "using cameras, random screenings, and sophisticated sensors" to pull in information. (They point admiringly to London's forty thousand security cameras.[52]) By taking this "broken windows" approach to counterterrorism, the police can leverage minor infractions, vague suspicions, and even routine contact into useful intelligence: "When it comes to recognizing suspicious behavior, U.S. law enforcement can learn much from the Israeli police. When the Israelis come into contact with criminal suspects, they ask such questions as: Why are you in Israel? How long have you been here? Where are you staying?—and then watch for behavioral responses."[53]

But this approach may require a shift in police priorities: "Prosecution of the case is less important than gathering intelligence and putting it into a database. No incident should be considered too minor for interaction with potential terrorists and for the collection of intelligence."[54]

Part Three: Gang Wars

From California to Afghanistan

The use of counterinsurgency in the "War on Terror"—both in the United States and abroad—built directly on strategies and practices that police have tested and refined in their campaigns against gangs.

In the summer of 2010, seventy marines from Camp Pendleton spent a week accompanying Los Angeles police in preparation for deployment to Afghanistan. The marines wanted to learn the basics of antigang investigations, standards of police professionalism, and techniques for building rapport with the community.[55]

A *New York Times* profile of Marine captain Scott Cuomo gives some idea of what he learned in L.A. and how he applied it in the combat zone: "The same Marines patrolled in the same villages each day, getting to recognize the residents. They awarded the elders construction projects and over hours of tea drinking showed them photographs they had taken of virtually every grown male in their battle space. 'Is this guy Taliban?' the Marines asked repeatedly, then poured what they learned into a computer database."

After a couple months, their efforts paid off. A villager identified a suspect, and the marines raided his house, arresting him and seizing weapons and opium. They placed the man, Juma Khan, in "a holding pen the size of a large dog cage" and interrogated him for two days. The marines then tried him and found him guilty of working with the Taliban. But under an agreement with local elders, once Khan swore allegiance to the new Afghan government, he was released as a free man—or not quite.

In exchange for his freedom and a job cleaning a nearby canal, Khan would be supervised by a group of elders who in turn reported to the U.S. military. And he himself became an informer, meeting regularly with the marines and answering their questions about his neighbors and friends.[56]

From Afghanistan to California

Again we see the lines of influence moving in both directions. Marines train with cops to prepare themselves for the work of managing a military occupation, and, at the same time, military lessons are battle-tested overseas and cycled back into the homeland.

Beginning in February 2009, combat veterans from Iraq and Afghanistan served as advisors to police in Salinas, California, with the stated aim of applying counterinsurgency tools to local anti-gang efforts.[57] Along with their expertise, advisors from the Naval Postgraduate School arrived with software, including a computer program to map the connections between gang activity, individual suspects, and their social circles, family ties, and neighborhood connections.[58]

This police-military partnership occurred simultaneously with a renewal and expansion of the Salinas Police Department's community policing efforts.[59] The new community focus (encouraged by the naval advisors) included Spanish-language training, an anonymous tip hotline, senior citizen volunteer programs, a larger role for the Police Community Advisory Council, parenting classes taught by officers, and youth programs.[60] The SPD took control of a community center in the Hebbron Heights neighborhood and stationed two officers there, assigned to perform foot patrols and focus on minor quality-of-life issues. More important than the direct police presence, however, were the coordination and intelligence-sharing between various nonprofits, government agencies, and the police.

The police actively sought to build a coalition including "the faith-based community, . . . all the social service agencies, educational institutions, the library, recreational services, . . . community organizations, [and] county and state agencies," in order to "establish a sense of trust" and "ultimately receive more information about community activity."[61] The thirty-four members of the "cross-functional team" (CFT) of the Community Alliance for Safety and Peace met regularly to share information, discuss emerging problems, and plan a coordinated response.[62] As a report from the National Council on Crime and Delinquency (NCCD) explains, the CFT first sought to "identify youth in Hebbron Heights most at risk for being victims or perpetrators of violence" and then "work[ed] to provide these youth and their families with as many protective factors as possible to reduce their risk of violence."[63] To make their assessments and draft their plans for intervention, team members "collect[ed] a variety of data about each client, including basic demographic information; school discipline data; probation/police data; and client connections or relationships with other CFT clients, local gangs, and extended family members." Twice each month, "CFT members collaboratively review[ed] the cases of targeted youth and their families in detail in order to determine the services and actions that [could] best provide support."[64] In principle, this process made additional services available to at-risk youth, but, equally, it enlisted social workers and teachers to help identify suspects for police investigations.

Alongside their community partnerships, Salinas police were also coordinating with other local, state, and federal law enforcement agencies, including the U.S. Marshals Service, the ATF (Alcohol, Tobacco, and Firearms), the FBI, and Immigration and Customs Enforcement.[65] The most spectacular product of these collaborations was a set of coordinated raids on April 22, 2010, codenamed Operation Knockout. The raids—coming after months of investigation—mobilized more than two hundred law enforcement agents and resulted in one hundred arrests, as well as the confiscation of forty pounds of cocaine, fourteen pounds of marijuana, and a dozen guns.[66]

Operation Knockout was intended not only to disrupt the targeted gangs but also to serve as a warning to others. Deputy Police Chief Kelly McMillin said: "We're going to follow quickly with call-ins of specific groups that we know are very active . . . . We are going to tell them that what happened on the 22nd could very well happen to them."[67]

The combination of social services and coercive force achieved a kind of coherence under a strategy called Operation Ceasefire. As the NCCD report explained: "Local goals of the program are to use data and intelligence to identify individuals at highest risk for committing firearms violence, then bring customized resources to those individuals to lead them away from violence; or, alternatively, to ensure these individuals are aware that if they choose to continue their violent tendencies they will be selected for rigorous law enforcement scrutiny and ultimately arrest and incarceration to ensure the community's safety."[68] In other words: behave and receive services, or misbehave and go to prison. The police came wielding both a carrot and a stick.

Slow Progress, Sudden Reversals

The results of Salinas's foray into counterinsurgency were

decidedly mixed. In the years following the partnership between the Naval Postgraduate School and the Salinas Police Department, the city's homicide rate leveled off, though it remained "substantially higher" than the state average.[69] Between 2011 and 2014, violent assaults fell by 18 percent. Overall firearms offenses dropped by 44 percent.[70] The portion of gun crime that was considered gang-related fell from 56 percent in 2012 to 10 percent in 2014.[71]

The community-building efforts also seemed to be having some effect. The NCCD review found "greater trust and confidence in the police" and a "more positive relationship between police officers and community members."[72] However, the researchers did note several causes for concern.[73] For instance, some people expressed what the NCCD euphemistically termed "confusion about the role of community police officers," usually arising after "family members were arrested by the same officers who were offering them services." As one client served by the Community Alliance for Safety and Peace so sharply put it, "We trusted them, but instead, they kick people out of their homes."[74]

If "confusion" was the problem, clarity arrived in 2014 when Salinas police shot and killed four Latino men in a period of just five months. (The city had previously averaged one police shooting per year.)[75] The public responded with widespread demonstrations, some of them violent, and with vocal accusations of racism and brutality.[76] Suddenly, all the goodwill that had been so carefully accumulated over the previous five years evaporated, community anger again became visible, and the cops' commitment to their "partnerships" was shown to be painfully thin.

At the request of the police chief, the U.S. Department of Justice (DOJ) Community Oriented Policing Service conducted a review of the Salinas Police Department and found numerous problems with their use-of-force policy, training, and internal investigations.[77] It also found "problems with respect for, as well as treatment and understanding of, many members of the Hispanic community."[78] Ultimately, the DOJ concluded, "The SPD lacks a unified, overarching community-collaborative policing philosophy and strategy."[79]

As if to prove the point, the following year both Hebbron Heights outreach officers were reassigned to regular patrol duty.[80]

Ceasefire, Compstat, COIN

Salinas's Operation Ceasefire—the centerpiece for its gang strategy—was an adaptation of a program developed in Boston under the same name.

In 1996, Boston's Ceasefire began with a focus on illegal handguns but soon broadened its attention to include the gangs that used them. In response to ongoing gang conflict, the Boston Police Department convened a working group consisting of law enforcement officers, social workers, academics, and members of the Black clergy.[81]

Researchers working with police created a list of 155 murders, mapping the crimes geographically and demographically. They examined the criminal records of both the victims and the assailants (where known). Using this information, they created a map of various gangs, their territory, and conflict points.[82]

Prioritizing the likely trouble spots, police officers then sat down with gang members and gave them a clear choice: if there was gang violence in their area, both the cops and the district attorney were going to hit with everything they had:

> They could disrupt street drug activity, focus police attention on low-level street crimes such as trespassing and public drinking, serve outstanding warrants, cultivate confidential informants for medium- and long-term investigations of gang activities, deliver strict probation and parole enforcement, seize drug proceeds and other assets, ensure stiffer plea bargains and sterner prosecutorial attention, request stronger bail terms (and enforce them), and even focus potentially severe federal investigative and prosecutorial attention on, for example, gang-related drug activity.[83]

On the other hand, if the gang members wanted to clean up their act, the police would help them do so. Because of their coalition work, the cops came with offers of job training, drug counseling, and other services.[84] In this respect, Operation Ceasefire grew directly from the Boston Police Department's pre-existing community policing programs.

The strategy worked through direct deterrence, denying the benefits of violence and raising the costs. As importantly, "Those costs were borne by the whole gang, not just the shooter."[85] So the cops could begin applying meaningful pressure before identifying a suspect, and the gang had an incentive to keep their members under control and maintain the peace.

The key elements of Operation Ceasefire—social network analysis, community partnerships, interagency cooperation, and a direct approach to deterrence—were quickly replicated and taken further in other cities, intersecting with trends like zero-tolerance policing and the Compstat program. A report from the Justice Department's Office of Community Oriented Policing Service, *Street Gangs and Interventions: Innovative Problem Solving with Network Analysis*, provides a case study illustrating the result.

In the mid-1990's, Newark's police were being remolded according to the pattern set by Giuliani's New York. The director of the Newark Police Department, Joe Santiago, introduced a Compstat system and in 1996 proposed a partnership with Rutgers University professor George Kelling. Slowly, Santiago built a working group including cops, scholars, social workers, the clergy, and even public defense attorneys. This partnership, the Greater Newark Safer Cities Initiative (GNSCI), began by focusing on a small number of repeat offenders, using the same deterrence model developed in Ceasefire. Then, in 2003, GNSCI turned its attention to gangs, leading it to look beyond the city limits. The North Jersey Gang Task Force was born.[86]

Coordinating with law enforcement agencies statewide, the Rutgers researchers began to collect a wide array of data on gang membership, recent crimes, recruitment practices, family ties, and so on—as well as "information on the criminal histories of all identified gang members." Once the data set was assembled, the researchers, following Boston's example, used it to map gang territory and perform a social network analysis, illustrating rivalries and alliances and identifying likely sites for conflict. They then took the analysis to the individual level, charting the connections between gang members and others who associated with them. By diagramming these relationships, researchers were able to distinguish between core members and those only marginally involved.[87]

Such information was crucial for making both tactical and strategic decisions. Police could approach particular members differently, based on their role in the gang and their level of commitment. And they could identify the pressure points and know where to strike for maximum effect. "Network analysis also allows one to identify people who hold structurally important positions within the gang networks. Cut points, people who are the only connection among people or groups of people, may be ideal selections for spreading a deterrence message or for affecting the structure and organization of the street gangs."[88]

Unlike Boston, where the focus was strictly on stopping gang *violence*, in New Jersey the aim was to disrupt the gangs themselves.

Carrots and Sticks, Hearts and Minds

Under the cost-benefit approach to counterinsurgency, the government provides an admixture of incentives and deterrents to shape the choices of its adversaries, their supporters, and the population as a whole. Simply put, the state creates a strategy to raise the costs associated with continued resistance and to reward cooperation. If the government can bring more force to bear and offer better rewards than the insurgents, rational self-interest should (in theory) lead people to side with the state rather than the rebels.[89] Ceasefire applied this same thinking to gangs.

At the same time, in developing Ceasefire, the police made sure to align other sources of legitimacy—social services, community organizations, the clergy—with their efforts, thus simultaneously increasing their leverage and heading off potential resistance. For example, in Boston, the Ceasefire coalition included Black ministers who had been vocal critics of the police. These men of the cloth began advising the cops in their antigang work and eventually "sheltered the police from broad public criticism."[90]

The other major approach to COIN—the older and more famous "hearts and minds" strategy—operates by a somewhat different logic, focusing on "the problems of modernization and the insurgent need for popular support." As RAND researchers explain, the aim was to rebuild public confidence in the government by instituting reforms, reducing corruption, and improving the population's standard of living.[91]

We can see the "hearts and minds" approach employed in a separate domestic experiment—the Justice Department's Weed and Seed program. Weed and Seed was conceived in 1991 and gained prominence a year later as part of the federal response to widespread rioting after the acquittal of four Los Angeles cops who had been videotaped beating Black motorist Rodney King. Since that time, it has been implemented in over three hundred neighborhoods nationwide.

The Department of Justice describes the project:

> The Weed and Seed strategy is based on a two-pronged approach:
>
> 1. Law enforcement agencies and criminal justice officials cooperate with local residents to "weed out" criminal activity in the designated area.
>
> 2. Social service providers and economic revitalization efforts are introduced to "seed" the area, ensuring long-term positive change and a higher quality of life for residents.[92]

In terms of strategy, Weed and Seed closely resembles the military's "Clear-Hold-Build." As the U.S. Army's counterinsurgency field manual 3-24, elaborates: "Create a secure physical and psychological environment. Establish firm government control of the populace and area. Gain the populace's support."[93]

Clearing and *holding* refer to the removal and exclusion of hostile elements. *Building*, on the other hand, means both literally repairing infrastructure and, more metaphorically, gaining trust and winning support. However, even *building* includes an element of force: "Progress in building support for the HN [Host Nation] government requires protecting the local populace . . . . To protect the populace, HN security forces continuously conduct patrols and use measured force against insurgent targets of opportunity . . . . Actions to eliminate the remaining covert insurgent political infrastructure must be continued."[94]

The domestic analogy is pretty straightforward. One police chief described the role of paramilitary units in his community policing strategy: "[The] only people that are going to be able to deal with these problems are highly trained tactical teams with proper equipment to go into a neighborhood and clear the neighborhood and hold it; allowing community policing officers to come in and start turning the neighborhood around."[95] In such campaigns, the relationship between community policing and militarization is especially clear. They're not competing or contradictory approaches. They work together, simultaneously or in series. One does the weeding, the other the seeding.

The implications are not lost on those subject to this sort of campaign. "They're gunning for us," Omari Salisbury, a Seattle teenager, said when he heard about Weed and Seed. "They're gunning for Black youth."[96]

Antigang Politics

Police antigang campaigns typically combine a variety of elements analogous to those in counterinsurgency: the creation of databases listing suspected gang members; the mapping of the social environment, illustrating connections between gang members, associates, families, et cetera; and the development of community contacts, especially with local leaders. These intelligence efforts are then paired with a campaign of persistent low-level harassment—stops, searches, petty citations, and the like. Each instance of harassment offers police the opportunity to collect additional information on the gang network while at the same time creating an inhospitable environment for those associated with gang activity.

For example, the main group responsible for keeping the pressure on gangs in Salinas was the Monterey County Gang Task Force, called "The Black Snake" by youths in the community. The task force had seventeen members, drawn from local police and sheriff's departments, the California Highway Patrol, and the Department of Corrections. Wearing distinctive black uniforms and driving black cars, task force members conducted mass-arrest "round-ups."[97] They made random traffic stops and regularly searched the homes of gang members on parole or probation.[98] The sheer volume of such activity was astonishing. In its first five years of operation, the task force was responsible for twenty-one thousand vehicle or pedestrian stops, five thousand parole and probation "compliance" searches, and twenty-eight hundred arrests.[99]

Such antigang efforts are always implicitly political, especially as they become permanent features of life in poor Black and Latino communities. Though ostensibly aimed at preventing gang violence, counter-gang campaigns inevitably lead police to monitor the community as a whole. A Fresno cop explained the intended scope of his department's gang files: "If you're twenty-one, male, living in one of these neighborhoods, been in Fresno for ten years and you're *not* in our computer—then there's definitely a problem."[100] Disproportionate attention, especially when paired with lower—or "zero"—tolerance for disorder, then contributes to higher rates of arrest and incarceration.[101]

Sometimes officials extend enforcement by securing gang injunctions, special court orders prohibiting activities that would otherwise be legal—barring alleged gang members from appearing together in public, restricting the clothing they can wear, and sub-jecting them to a nighttime curfew.[102] At a broader level, the po-lice will often engage in efforts disrupting ordinary social life in gang-affected areas, such as cordoning, saturating, or sweeping se-lect locations (e.g., parks, streets, or bars) or targeted events (ball-games, parties, car shows).[103]

In the most advanced campaigns, police sometimes take the fur-ther step of strategically *causing* gang conflict. Following the 1992 Los Angeles riots, for example, police did what they could to wreck a city-wide truce between the Bloods and the Crips. The cops at-tacked negotiating meetings and inter-gang social events and also engaged in some underhanded tactics to create friction: covering one gang's graffiti with another's or arresting a Blood only to release him deep in Crip territory. This occurred not only in a context of widespread anger and recent unrest, but also at a point at which the gangs themselves were becoming increasingly politicized.[104]

Mike Davis described the government's response to the riots in military terms: "In Los Angeles I think we are beginning to see a repressive context that is literally comparable to Belfast or the West Bank, where policing has been transformed into full-scale counter-insurgency . . . against an entire social stratum or ethnic group."[105]

Part Four: Preserving Order, Preventing Change

Co-optation and Coercion

Thus far, I have focused mainly on the "hard" side of repres-sion—the direct coercion, the forceful disruptions, the criminal-ization and incarceration, the violence. But we need to look also at the "soft" side—those elements which at this point are typical of the state's response to opposition from the left: the strategic use of concessions, the promise of representation and access, the co-optation of leadership, and, comprising all of these, the institu-tionalization of dissent.[106] By these means, the state does not only achieve control and exercise power *over* the organizations of the left but also *through* them.

One RAND researcher argues: "The ideal allies for a government implementing control are, in fact, nonviolent members of the community the would-be insurgents seek to mobilize . . . . If regimes can infiltrate—or, better yet, cooperate with—mainstream groups they are often able to gain information on radical activities and turn potential militants away from violence."[107]

Broadly speaking, counterinsurgency offers two approaches to dealing with opposition, and they must be used selectively. Some adversaries, especially moderates, may be co-opted, bought off, and appeased. Others, the more recalcitrant portion, must be forcefully disorganized, disrupted, deterred, or destroyed. The balance of concessions and coercion will be apportioned accordingly.

Some adversaries win new posts—offices in a "reformed" administration or jobs in "responsible" nonprofits, labor unions, or progressive think tanks. They gain access, inclusion, or representation in exchange for working within the existing institutional framework. The others will face harsher outcomes—including, for example, imprisonment, exile, or assassination. Whatever the approach in a particular case, the important thing is that the opposition is neutralized—rendered harmless, made controllable, and exploited as either the object or the tool of state power.

Salinas again provides an unusually clear example. There the police did not merely co-opt existing leadership but went further, selecting and developing their own community leaders. The Community Alliance for Safety and Peace organized a "Leadership Academy," in which select community members would receive training in "team building, conflict resolution, project management, leadership, public speaking, advocacy, and resource development." As part of their training, the future leaders were then "encouraged to start a community group with the purpose of improving their neighborhood." Some formed groups to "support witnesses of crimes, connect parents to educational institutions, connect youth to services and recreation programs, [and] beautify areas and reduce 'broken windows.'"[108] In this way, the police helped create the leaders and organizations that would support their mission and help build the kind of popular support needed for police legitimacy.

"Force Multipliers": The Military-NGO Complex

Counterinsurgency theory places a heavy emphasis on shaping the social environment in which the population lives and resistance develops. One way governments exercise this influence is with their money. As FM 3-24 explains: "*Some of the Best Weapons for Counterinsurgents Do Not Shoot*. . . . Counterinsurgents often achieve the most meaningful success in garnering public support and legitimacy for the HN government with activities that do not involve killing insurgents. . . . [L]asting victory comes from a vibrant economy, political participation, and restored hope. Particularly after security has been achieved, dollars and ballots will have more important effects than bombs and bullets . . . 'money is ammunition.'"[109] Foreign aid has thus often been criticized as an instrument of imperialism, even when the funds are distributed indirectly through nongovernmental organizations (NGOs) or nongovernmental humanitarian organizations (NGHOs).[110]

As the United States began its war against Afghanistan in October 2001, Secretary of State Colin Powell—the former general and the founding chairman of the nonprofit America's Promise Alliance—managed to embarrass NGO leaders with his praise for their work. Speaking at the National Foreign Policy Conference for Leaders of Nongovernmental Organizations, he said: "Just as surely as our diplomats and military, American NGOs are out there serving and sacrificing on the front lines of freedom. . . . [NGOs] are such a force multiplier for us, such an important part of our combat team."[111]

Later, guidelines negotiated by representatives of the military and the major humanitarian groups discouraged any repetition of Powell's gaffe, specifying that "U.S. Armed Forces should not describe NGHOs as 'force multipliers' or 'partners' of the military."[112] FM 3-24 managed to retain Powell's meaning while avoiding the offensive language: "Many such agencies resist being overtly involved with military forces," it cautions; but then: "some kind of liaison [is] needed. . . to ensure that, as much as possible, objectives are shared and actions and messages synchronized."[113]

The RAND study *Networks and Netwars* outlines "a range of possibilities" for the military's use of international nonprofits, "from encouraging the early involvement of appropriate NGO networks in helping to detect and head off a looming crisis, to working closely with them in the aftermath of conflicts to improve the effectiveness of U.S. forces still deployed, to reduce the residual hazards they face, and to strengthen the often fragile peace."[114] One result of this perspective is that aid money, and thus NGO attention, increasingly follows the state's priorities—and its military's priorities in particular.[115]

For instance, in 2010 the United States awarded $114 million to aid groups working in Yemen, with the stated goal of "improving the livelihood of citizens in targeted communities and improving governance capabilities."[116] This supposedly humanitarian assistance came alongside $1.2 billion in military aid, clandestine military and intelligence activity, and a CIA assessment that the Al Qaeda affiliate in Yemen represented the largest threat to U.S. global security.[117] General David Petraeus was frank in referring the U.S. involvement in the country as "Preventive Counterinsurgency Operations."[118]

The following year, the United States continued to provide military aid and development assistance and escalated its covert military actions—including the controversial assassination of the cleric Anwar al Awlaki (an American citizen)—even as the State Department expressed concern over the Yemeni government's brutal repression of a popular Arab Spring uprising.[119]

As the military invests more deeply in "nation-building" projects, and as humanitarian assistance finds itself militarized, the distinctions between military and development aid are becoming increasingly irrelevant.[120] Writing in the *New Republic*, David Rieff concludes: "Development is a continuation of war by other means."[121]

No Justice, Urban Peace

The domestic counterpart to the nongovernmental "force multiplier" is the community policing "partnership." We've seen nonprofit funding tied to the criminal justice agenda in the Weed and Seed program; the use of social services and Black churches to create "the 'network of capacity' necessary to legitimize, fund, equip, and carry out" Boston's Operation Ceasefire; the collaboration of social workers, the clergy, and public defense attorneys for similar ends in Newark; police-trained community leaders in Salinas; and in Los Angeles a plan to use social service agencies to gain access to Muslim communities suspected of breeding terrorists.[122]

But sometimes police-led partnerships go further, using progressive nonprofits to channel and control political opposition, moving it in safe, institutional, and reformist directions, rather than toward more radical or militant action. For example, consider the efforts of liberal nonprofits to contain community anger after transit police shot and killed an unarmed Black man in Oakland, California. Oscar Grant was killed on January 1, 2009. A week later, on January 7, a protest against the police turned into a small riot.[123] Organizers with the Coalition Against Police Executions (CAPE)—a group largely composed of progressive nonprofits and Black churches—denounced the crowd's violence. One CAPE leader said that he wept watching the riots on television, feeling that years of hard work were being "destroyed by anarchists."[124] But—likely because of the revolt—the cop in the case, Johannes Mehserle, was arrested and charged with murder.

Before the riots there had been no statement of concern from the mayor's office, no Justice Department investigation, and no arrests. In fact, Mehserle's employers had not even interviewed him about the incident. "The rebellion was really about the fact that nothing was being done," George Ciccariello-Maher explains. "If there's one lesson to take from this, it's that the only reason Mehserle was arrested is because people tore up the city. It was the riot—and the threat of future riots."[125]

In an effort to reassert its leadership, CAPE organized another demonstration for January 14. Speakers included Mayor Ron Dellums, the rapper Too $hort, and representatives of various nonprofits—all of whom urged the crowd to remain peaceful. Furthermore, CAPE's designated marshals, operating under the supervision of a private security guard, surrounded the demonstration while unidentified informants mingled in the crowd to look for troublemakers.[126] Despite the tight control, things did not go as planned. When the speeches were over, much of the crowd refused to leave. Organizers announced that police would intervene if the group would not disperse; but, rather than wait, CAPE's own marshals formed a line and began pushing people off the streets. The crowd—now very angry—started breaking windows. The security team, after consulting with police, withdrew from the area and left it to the cops to handle the crowd. The police fired tear gas and made arrests.[127]

Future demonstrations, beginning on January 30, were likewise handled with threats, arrests, and violence.[128] At the same time, and in keeping with the COIN model, local, state, and federal agencies all undertook extensive intelligence operations targeting protest organizers—monitoring websites, videotaping crowds, sending plainclothes officers into the demonstrations, and infiltrating planning meetings.[129]

"If we learned on January seventh that our power was in the streets," Ciccariello-Maher concludes, "what we learned on the fourteenth is that the state was going to counter-attack. . . . The state didn't counterattack by force at first; the state counterattacked through these institutions, the nonprofits."[130]

A year later, the process repeated itself. As Johannes Mehserle's trial approached, Nicole Lee, director of the nonprofit Urban Peace

Movement, circulated an email focused not on winning justice but on preventing violence should justice be denied. Titled "Bracing for Mehserle Verdict: Community Engagement Plan," the June 23, 2010, memo offered two sets of instructions:

1) Organizations, CBO's [community-based organizations], and Public Agencies should be thinking of ways to *create organized events or avenues for young people and community members to express their frustrations with the system* in constructive and peaceful ways. If people have no outlets then it may be easier for folks to be pulled toward more destructive impulses.

2) We need to *begin "inoculating" our bases and the community at-large so that when the verdict comes down, people are prepared* for it, and so that the "outside agitators" who were active during the initial Oscar Grant protests are not able to incite the crowd so easily.[131]

The memo listed several talking points, which served the state's interests so well that the City of Oakland ran an edited version on its website.[132]

Around the same time, another organization, ironically named Youth Uprising, sponsored a public service announcement centered on the slogan "Violence is not justice." The video featured local rappers, civil rights attorneys, school administrators, representatives from nonprofits, a police captain, and the district attorney of San Francisco—all urging a peaceful response to the verdict.[133] Religious leaders also got into the act, using the pulpit to ask people to remain safely at home when the verdict was announced.[134]

The pacifying efforts, though broadly distributed, were centrally coordinated. Shortly before the trial, the mayor and police held a meeting with several Bay Area nonprofits. The topic, of course, was the prevention of riots.[135] In practice, avoiding unrest became the primary focus of the institutionalized left; CAPE's stated goal, the prevention of police brutality, receded into the background. If anything, by condemning the rioters and cooperating with the cops, liberal leaders helped to legitimize the police counter-attack and made further brutality more likely, not less.

In the end, Officer Mehserle was convicted but of a lesser charge—manslaughter, rather than murder. And, when the verdict was announced, rioting did ensue.[136] Hundreds of people, mostly young people of color, braved not only the clubs and the tear gas of the police but also the condemnation of their purported community leaders.[137]

Advance the Struggle

In their published analysis of the Oscar Grant crisis, the revolutionary group Advance the Struggle argued that, by trying to defuse popular anger, "Bay Area nonprofits effectively acted as an extension of the state."[138]

Had the rage over Grant's murder not been channeled into ritualized protest, had the leaders not been more concerned with controlling the community response than in confronting injustice, had the organizing not been, in a word, institutionalized—it is hard to know what might have been possible.

Advance the Struggle contrasted the trajectory of events in Oakland with those of Greece, just a few weeks before Grant's death: "There, the police murder of a 15-year-old Alexandros Grigoropoulos triggered reactions which, very quickly, evolved from protests to riots to a general strike in which 2.5 million workers were on strike in December 2008. Within days the killer cop and police accomplices were arrested, but even this concession didn't trick the movement into subsiding. The police murder set off the uprising, but the participants connected the murder with the issues of unemployment, neo-liberal economic measures, political corruption, and a failing education system. Aren't we facing similar problems in Oakland?"[139]

Of course there are differences between Oakland and Athens—differences of geography, history, and political culture. The type of insurrection unleashed in Greece may not have been possible in California. But that is not an *objection* to the radical analysis; it is, instead, *the premise*. The political environment in Oakland has been shaped in such a way so as to sharply limit the potential for struggle. And the institutionalization of conflict in professionalized nonprofits is an important part of that restrictive context. There is no guarantee that things would have gone further had the nonprofits not intervened, or that greater conflict would have won greater gains. But their intervention certainly helped to contain the rebellion and closed off untold possibilities for further action. That is quite clearly what it was intended to do.

Conclusion: Wartime

In this essay, I have tried to illustrate something of the transfer of counterinsurgency theory, strategy, technique, and personnel from the military to the police, and vice versa. I've shown how COIN has informed the government's wholesale surveillance of the American Muslim population, how antigang campaigns are both shaping and being shaped by military operations abroad, and how the state uses nongovernmental and nonprofit agencies, alongside military and police action, to channel and control opposition.

In this context, the chapter's title—"The Other Side of the COIN"—has three distinct meanings, which correspond to the main themes of my argument. First, it refers to the strategic pairing of direct coercion and subtle legitimacy-building activities. Second, it points to the joint development of military operations overseas and police control domestically. And third, it reminds us that when the authorities turn to counterinsurgency it is because they fear that insurgency is brewing.

Gangs, States, and Insurgencies

Prologue: A Credible Threat

In the spring of 2015, as Baltimore took its place in a wave of rioting precipitated by police violence, rival street gangs entered into a truce, pledging not to attack one another or engage in looting. The gangs quietly formulated some rules of engagement for the riot period, with specific protections for journalists and Black-owned businesses.[1] Gang members actively discouraged looting, broke up fights, and in one instance formed a line between protesters and police.[2]

The police reacted with their instinctual—or, rather, institutional—paranoia, issuing a press release headlined "Credible Threat to Law Enforcement." It flatly declared: "The Baltimore Police Department/Criminal Intelligence Unit has received credible information that members of various gangs including the Black Guerrilla Family, Bloods, and Crips have entered into a partnership to 'take-out' law enforcement officers. This is a *credible threat*."[3]

Gang leaders insisted that targeting police was never on the agenda.[4] Regardless, they were singled out and attacked by police during the demonstrations, even as they protected stores from looters. And in one absurdist scene, police pulled truce leaders out of bed and charged them with violating the emergency curfew.[5]

Interpreting these events is partly a matter of fitting them into an historical lineage. Many observers compared the Baltimore truce with an earlier one, from the period of the 1992 Los Angeles riots.[6] Some gang members look back even farther: "Our actual laws and bylaws are laws that are set for us by the Black Panthers, which is to protect and serve and to help out the community and make sure it's equal rights between everybody and it's always justice served."[7]

Interestingly, some who tried to extend the truce beyond the period of the uprising believed the key to peace lay in reestablishing the traditional gang hierarchy. "When I was coming up in neighborhoods," one Blood leader recalled, "the older cats were the gangsters who ran the neighborhood. They was the ones who kept the neighborhood in line, kept the youngsters in check. . . . There was a protocol you had to follow, you had rules you had to follow and the ones who ran the hood was the gangsters."[8]

At issue here are questions that extend beyond any one city, set, or uprising, and connect instead with the nature of gangs, states, and revolutions. To explore these questions, I will look at gangs as *political* actors. In so doing, I review several case studies drawn mainly from two distinct periods of gang politicization, the 1960s and the 1990s, and I examine the complex relations between various gangs and the Black Panther Party. But I begin by considering the state's strategy in suppressing gangs and what it may suggest about the challenges they pose.

Part One: Politicizing Gangs

Insurgent Gangs

Among the unanticipated consequences of the 2003 U.S. invasion of Iraq, we may count the growing recognition that American police employ the techniques of counterinsurgency against American street gangs. Hence, military advisors have consulted with local police departments, researchers have applied COIN methodology and Defense Department technology to the analysis of crime statistics, and returning veterans have applied the skills they gained in foreign campaigns to their new jobs in law enforcement.[9] This adaptation of counter*insurgency* warfare to *antigang* policing poses an important question: *are gangs insurgents?*

Some military theorists and police strategists clearly think that they are—at least some gangs, under certain conditions.[10] John Sullivan, an L.A. County sheriff's deputy, warns in one RAND Corporation report: "Some [gangs] have begun to adopt varying degrees of political activity. At the low end, this activity may include dominating neighborhood life and creating virtual 'lawless zones,' application of street taxes, or taxes on other criminal actors. Gangs with more sophisticated political attributes typically co-opt police and government officials to limit interference with their activities. At the high end, some gangs have active political agendas, using the political process to further their ends and destabilize governments."[11]

Among the examples Sullivan cites are the Gangster Disciples, a gang with thirty thousand members in thirty-five states. In addition to employing themselves in the drug trade, the Gangster Disciples fund a political action committee, "infiltrate police and private security agencies, sponsor political candidates, register voters, and sponsor protest marches." Likewise, another gang, the Unknown Conservative Vice Lords, "has embraced similar activities, including establishing a nonprofit political association known as the United Concerned Voters' League." At the extreme, he points to the Black P Stone Nation's 1986 plot to buy rocket-propelled grenades for a Qaddafi-funded terror campaign.[12]

Had Sullivan looked further into the past—as many gang members do—he would have been forced to admit that these forays into politics were nothing new.

The Vanguard of the Dispossessed

Historically, many of today's gangs began as protective measures against racist violence. L.A.'s first gang problem involved white gangs like the Spookhunters enforcing the city's de facto segregation and occasionally attacking Black neighborhoods. Black gangs emerged in the late 1940s as defensive bodies and then became increasingly politicized as a result of the 1965 Watts riots.[13] During that uprising, rival sets put aside their differences and fought together, and an informal ceasefire held for more than three years afterward.[14] Following the riots, one gang—the Slausons, the largest in Los Angeles at the time, boasting five thousand members—initiated the Community Alert Patrol; they followed the cops with cameras and notebooks a year before the Black Panthers began their armed patrols in Oakland. One Slauson, Ron Wilkins, became a leader of the local chapter of the Student Nonviolent Coordinating Committee. Another, Alprentice "Bunchy" Carter, founded the Los Angeles chapter of the Black Panther Party after meeting Eldridge Cleaver, the Panthers' minister of information, who was teaching an African American history and culture class in Soledad prison.[15]

Likewise, in Chicago, José "Cha Cha" Jiménez, a leader of the Puerto Rican street gang the Young Lords, pushed his group to take on more of a public service ethos, beginning in 1964. Then, after meeting Panther leader Fred Hampton in jail in 1968, Jiménez began modeling the Young Lords Organization on the Black Panther Party. The Young Lords created their own thirteen-point program, sponsored food and clothing giveaways, and offered free breakfasts for children.[16]

In this same period, in Chicago's Uptown neighborhood, a group of young people associated with JOIN (Jobs or Income Now) formed a semi-autonomous group called the Goodfellows. Historians Amy Sonnie and James Tracy describe it as "a cross between a street gang and a loose-knit radical social club." The Goodfellows opened a venue for bands and other social engagements and set out to unite and politicize the local gangs, specifically organizing against police brutality. They began a patrol to observe the police and document the abuse they witnessed, borrowing the idea from Community Alert in Los Angeles. Later, when JOIN folded, the Goodfellows, inspired by the example of the Panthers, formed the Young Patriots Organization, drafting their own ten-point program, opening community health clinics, and running a free breakfast program. Along with the Young Lords and the Chicago Indian Village, they fought against urban renewal and occupied government-owned buildings. They published a newspaper demanding the release of jailed Black Panthers, and they called on whites to abandon racism, act in solidarity with people of color, and "fight the real enemy."[17]

Under Fred Hampton's guidance, the Young Lords and the Young Patriots joined together with the Panthers in a "Rainbow Coalition," which he envisioned as the "vanguard of the dispossessed."[18] Or, as another Panther organizer, Bob Lee, later put it, "The Rainbow Coalition was just a code word for class struggle."[19]

War and Peace in the City of Angels

A generation later, another truce and another riot seemed to signal a new period of politicization. On March 27, 1992, just before the outbreak of rioting in response to the acquittal of the cops filmed beating Rodney King, four Los Angeles gangs signed a formal peace agreement modeled on the 1948 Arab-Israeli ceasefire. Articles I, II, and IV of the "Multi-Peace Treaty—General Armistice Agreement" called for an end to violence, established principles of non-aggression, and detailed the terms of the peace. Article III looked to the larger society to establish conditions under which peace would be sustainable, specifically "the return of black business, economic development and advancement of educational programs."[20] The treaty came after months of negotiations initiated by older gang members and the Coalition Against Police Abuse—a group founded by former Black Panthers working to keep the party's legacy alive while also learning from its mistakes.[21]

Gang violence declined at once. The homicide rate fell an astonishing 87.5 percent in truce areas.[22] Latino gangs soon made similar moves. La eMe (also known as the Mexican Mafia) and MS-13 (Mara Salvatrucha) declared an end to drive-by shootings, immediately reducing the citywide total by 25 percent.[23] By 1998, L.A.'s overall homicide rate had declined 36.7 percent.[24]

The police responded to the ceasefire by intensifying repression. They targeted truce leaders for surveillance, raids, arrests, and deportation. They also employed a variety of dirty tricks: spreading rumors to create distrust, snitch-jacketing leaders to provoke retaliation, and spray-painting one gang's tags over another's to spark conflict.[25]

For the state, the ceasefire represented a political problem. As the Los Angeles County Gang Task Force argued in one report: "The impact of gang truces on communities can be negative. A truce can reinforce the gang's identify. . . . [At] its worst, a truce serves to legitimize the identity of a gang and its members and lengthens its illegitimate reach."[26] Connie Rice, a civil rights lawyer who helped with the gang negotiations, eventually came to agree. In her memoir, she described the truce as "a bad idea" and "a big mistake," worrying that such efforts "mak[e] the gang stronger, more cohesive, and more attractive," ultimately "validating the gang's status." She now advises police departments on their campaigns against gangs, taking a counterinsurgency approach.[27]

It seems that however much the cops may dislike gang violence, they like gang peace even less. Whatever their limitations and contradictions, gangs in the period of rebellion represented an armed challenge to state control. So long as "banging" kept the gangs divided and thus weak, the public fear of gang violence could be leveraged into support for policing. "Trucing," in contrast, emphasized the gangs' common circumstances and, in the context of the riots, common enemies. Furthermore, the drop in violence brought the gangs a measure of community support, which was dangerous from the state's perspective—more so, apparently, than drive-by shootings.

Gangs and Legitimacy

Like all political actors, street gangs rely on a combination of force and legitimacy. In his seminal ethnographic study *Islands in the Street*, Martín Sánchez-Jankowski notes four things gangs need from the community: recruits, information, psychological support (approval, a sense of belonging, etc.), and most of all "a 'safe haven' from which to operate." In other words: "What the gang requires from the community is total noncooperation with law enforcement."[28] To acquire these needs, it is important to maintain some level of popular support, which requires in turn that the gang meet some important social need: "the community needs certain services that the gang provides. Probably the most important service that gangs can provide is protection."[29] Sánchez-Jankowski documents gangs offering protection against street crime (including other gangs), loan sharks, price gauging, gentrification, mafia-style racketeering, and threats to the ethnic or cultural character of the neighborhood.[30]

Though this relationship is reciprocally beneficial, it remains asymmetrical: "the gang is in need of the community more than the community is in need of the gang."[31] Therefore, it is only ever the community that has the power to directly dissolve the arrangement—either passively, through informal disapproval, withholding information, and discouraging recruitment, or actively, by going to the police. Such actions typically result from some dereliction on the part of the gang—either failing to provide protection or losing control of its own members.[32] The cops naturally seek to exploit such lapses, but they too rely on the public's support, and the balance can be difficult to maintain. For example, in the late 1980s, street battles over crack cocaine markets and the resulting epidemic of drive-by shootings created unusual levels of neighborhood support for the LAPD's aggressive tactics. This support, however, proved short-lived, as the siege-like atmosphere and regular brutality came to fuel resentments that would explode into rioting in 1992, after the acquittal of the police who beat Rodney King.[33]

Politicization and Depoliticization

In their profile of Los Solidos in Hartford, Connecticut, Albert DiChiara and Russell Chabot highlight the complexities of gang-community relations. In addition to selling drugs, the Solids (as they are called in English), promoted a Puerto Rican nationalist ideology and organized neighborhood cleanup days, sponsored youth sports teams, participated in food drives with local churches, joined with other gangs in a demonstration (and then riot) against discrimination in the construction industry, and provided "community coaches" to help gang youth earn their high school diplomas. The picture that emerges from the study, however, is that of an organization suffering from badly divided aims. The entrepreneurial (criminal) activities of Los Solidos helped to fund their community (political) programs and in some ways relied on the loyalty such efforts earned them. Nevertheless, drug dealing and its associated activities tended to undercut their neighborhood support. Then, in 1996, when several key leaders were arrested and sent to prison, the gang responded by "mov[ing] its activities underground"— withdrawing from community work, decentralizing its organization, and continuing drug sales.[34]

It is hard to know what this outcome might signify. The prosecutions seem to have depoliticized the gang. But how and why? One hypothesis is that the gang's community efforts were merely a front for their criminal activities, and when visibility became too costly they dropped the politics in favor of low-profile drug dealing. Another possible explanation is that the police campaign removed the gang's political leadership but left its criminal and commercial infrastructure more or less intact. Did the prosecutions change the nature of the organization or merely alter its behavior? Or, looking at it from a different angle: were the Solids using their political activities to serve their business interests or using their criminal enterprise to advance their social agenda?[35] Obviously, to some degree they were doing both, but the difference remains an important one. It may be that one way of distinguishing between gangsters and revolutionaries is by examining their priorities—in particular, how they behave when their economic project conflicts with their political objectives.

New Kings

A similar dilemma and, sadly, a similar outcome are apparent in David Brotherton and Luis Barrios's extensive study of New York's Almighty Latin King and Queen Nation (ALKQN). Beginning in 1995, following an intense power struggle within the gang, a new leader, King Tone (Antonio Fernández), embarked on an effort to take the group in a new, more political direction, inspired in large part by the historical examples of the Black Panthers and their Puerto Rican allies, the Young Lords.[36] In the late 1990s, ALKQN began publicly participating in a range of demonstrations, including the Million Man March, the National AIDS Walk, and New York's annual Puerto Rico Day parade.[37] At the same time, they started offering tutoring services, AIDS education, addiction recovery support groups, and domestic violence counseling.[38]

Comparing the periods before and during King Tone's leadership, the researchers noted differences in both the structure and culture of the ALKQN. After King Tone took over, the gang became less centralized and less territorial. Conflicts were settled more through negotiation and mediation, with violence as only a last resort. The group abolished its use of the death penalty, removed the violent element from its initiation rituals, relied less on intimidation for discipline, and adopted procedural safeguards for resolving disputes and punishing those who violated the gang's rules. Ideologically, ALKQN grew more spiritual, community--minded, and even utopian. The group became more supportive of education and self-improvement and less tolerant of delinquency and crime. Perhaps most interesting, it began taking deliberate steps toward greater gender equality.[39]

Between 1996 and 1999, researchers could find *no* homicides as a result of internal conflict and at most four assaults resulting in injury. A strict rule against retaliation likewise reduced inter-gang conflict. During the same period, there was but a single homicide involving a Latin King, and he was the victim, not the aggressor.[40]

This more peaceful, socially conscious direction, Brotherton and Barrios note, brought several advantages to the ALKQN, including feelings of personal empowerment, a sense of historical continuity with earlier social movements, legitimacy in the eyes of the community, and support from the political left.[41] What it did not provide, however, was a respite from police harassment.

In 1999, King Tone was imprisoned on drug charges, and his attempt to reinvent the ALKQN abruptly disintegrated: "The group fell into a state of confusion and disorientation; no solid political power base emerged that could continue to take the group forward on the same communitarian path of reform. The absence of any new credible leadership produced the conditions for the group to splinter into local spheres of influence that often reverted to the practices of the group prior to its reform years."[42]

Looking back on this defeat, Brotherton and Barrios identified "a number of structural problems with the organization" that made possible such a dramatic reversal. These included 1) its hierarchical organization, "which left it vulnerable when the leadership was removed by the state"; 2) a lack of community support and resources; 3) infiltration by "'snitches' and provocateurs"; 4) the absence of "a larger radical movement developing in the surrounding community"; and 5) the persistence of a "gangsta mentality."[43]

King Tone's efforts, while in many respects admirable, fell short of the minimum changes necessary to achieve his vision for the ALKQN's new role, and for the broader objective of winning freedom for the Puerto Rican community. As journalist, historian, and former Young Lord Juan Gonzáles observed, "The Latin Kings were children of the Young Lords. . . . The Kings had a lot of the same sort of radical wrath we had back then. . . . [But the Kings] were really a gang that leaders tried to turn into a political group, and they could never master the transformation."[44]

For a gang to create a revolution, it is also necessary to revolutionize the gang.

Part Two: Crime as Politics

Black Power in the Black Market

Sometimes the economic project is the political program.

In the sixties, the economic position of Black gangs was partly a result of discrimination in the legal economy, which pressed many young men toward illegal work, and partly the result of discrimination in the underground economy, which relegated Blacks to the lowest level of the criminal hierarchy. Following the logic of "Black capitalism," establishment figures like the economist Robert Browne and congressional representatives Adam Clayton Powell and William Dawson identified Black control of the illicit economy as a worthy aim.[45] Likewise, the Congress of Racial Equality passed a resolution in 1967 affirming that "Blacks should take control of the operation of vices in their community, should turn them into economic enterprises, and should eliminate those most harmful to the psychological health of the community."[46]

One group that pursued this aim with a persistent focus and at times considerable success, was the Blackstone Rangers—later the Black P Stone Nation and then the El Rukns. Historians Joshua Bloom and Waldo Martin write: "From their start in the early 1960s, the Rangers had focused on community building as an adjunct to their illegal activities, which included drug trafficking and extortion. As a result, they constituted a sort of parallel government on the South Side [of Chicago], protecting members of their neighborhood from other gangs and from police and providing some community services."[47]

The Rangers organized cultural activities like jazz concerts and plays and operated a youth center and a restaurant.[48] They consciously borrowed elements from the Black Power movement: the colors red, black, and green; the pyramid symbol, recalling ancient Egypt; Afro hairstyles; and admiration for figures like Malcolm X, Stokely Carmichael, H. Rap Brown, and Panther founders Huey Newton and Bobby Seale. They insisted that the members study Black history and advocated the founding of an independent Black nation.[49] The group published a newspaper covering the civil rights movement, policing, political repression, and unemployment in the Black community.[50] Though superficially very different from one another, these various areas of activity—cultural, community-minded, and criminal—may yet have represented a coherent program. "In a sense," historian Will Cooley reasons, "taking over these rackets was a political objective, compatible with the 'community control' mantra."[51]

Money and Politics

In their earliest years, the Rangers served as street muscle and errand-runners for older, more established Black crime bosses. In the late sixties, though, that dependency was broken by an influx of federal money.[52] In 1967, the Office of Economic Opportunity (OEO) issued the Woodlawn Organization a grant totaling $927,341 for an educational and job-training program both serving and employing the members of two rival gangs—the Rangers and the Disciples. The program placed 105 people in jobs, 65 of whom remained employed in those positions one year later. More significantly, gang-related murders declined 44 percent in the program area, as neither group wanted to jeopardize their federal funding.[53] However, corruption was rife in the program, and it was eventually revealed that its administrators had forged signatures on hundreds of checks, defrauding the government of thousands of dollars. In 1972, Ranger leader Jeff Fort and four others went to prison for fraud, forgery, and conspiracy.[54]

In 1976, Fort returned from prison to announce a new direction for his organization. Henceforth the core of the Black Stone Nation would be known as El Rukn, and its focus would be religion, education, and Black Nationalism.[55] The Rukns organized against police brutality, unemployment, and slumlords. The group's leaders held court and adjudicated disputes in its "Moorish temple," handling problems ranging from family discord to auto accidents. They tried to organize gang truces but were frustrated in these efforts, partly because of standing grievances and partly because of FBI interference. They also sponsored voter registration drives, which pulled the organization into the orbit of the Democratic Party machine. In 1983, the group was paid $10,000 to flier on behalf of Mayor Jane Byrne's reelection campaign. Rukns also assembled in large numbers outside of polling places to intimidate opposition voters.[56] Soon after, the Rukns' relationship with the Nation of Islam brought them into contact with Muammar Qaddafi, a connection that ultimately led Jeff Fort back to prison. Fort had offered the gang's services as the shock troops in a Libyan-funded terrorism campaign—though, as Natalie Y. Moore and Lance Williams persuasively argue in *The Almighty Black P Stone Nation*, it is more likely that his intention was not to carry out the attacks but to cheat Qaddafi out of millions of dollars.[57]

This rather mixed political history extended to the Rangers' contact with the civil rights movement. In 1965, Rangers served as bodyguards for Martin Luther King Jr. and argued with him about the efficacy of nonviolence over a game of pool. In the summer of 1966, hundreds of Rangers made a dramatic appearance at a rally against housing discrimination.[58] Later, along with the Vice Lords and the Disciples, they participated in demonstrations led by Jesse Jackson, against discrimination in the construction industry.[59] After King's assassination, the Rangers organized nonviolent protests and even took over a high school assembly to warn the students against rioting.[60]

But the Blackstone Rangers also extorted money from civil rights groups, provided security for grocery stores when they were picketed by Jesse Jackson's Operation Breadbasket, and very likely burned down a church after a sermon denouncing gang activity and the Rangers' influence specifically. As a result, they alienated many of their political allies and much of the Black community.[61]

Crime as Repression

Perhaps more strange was the Rangers' relationship to the authorities.

Every summer from 1966 to 1968, gang leaders worked with the cops to keep Chicago's Woodlawn neighborhood quiet.[62] As Fort stated in the *Chicago Daily Defender*: "We don't want a riot . . . we've been working with the police trying to keep down incidents that might lead to a riot."[63] During periods of tension and unrest, the Rangers sold businesses placards reading "DO NOT Touch—Black P Stones—Jeff," charging $100 for each sign. Both the Woodlawn Business Association and the Jackson Park Business Association publicly credited the Rangers with helping "cool things down."[64]

Such alliances were, of course, in the background of the decision to make federal money available to the street gangs. As OEO project manager Jerome S. Bernstein testified before a Senate subcommittee: "These two youth gangs [the Rangers and the Disciples] were responsible for preventing a Black Panther meeting on August 1, 1967 which was to be held on the West Side of Chicago for the express purpose of forging a coalition of youth gangs to collectively 'take on the City' during the summer of 1967. These two gangs proclaimed that there would be no riots and that there would be no Black Panther meeting. There were no riots and there was no Black Panther meeting."[65]

J. Sakai is unsparing in his judgment of this arrangement, describing the Blackstone Rangers and Disciples as "mercenaries" hired by the government and bribed "with 'poverty grants' to violently repress 'riots' and all other Black community anti-capitalist activity."[66]

Three Strategies: Suppression, Co-optation, and Encapsulation

Don Hamerquist, a communist organizer active in Chicago and

close to many of the events described here, argues that rather than a "coherent and unified 'government policy,'" there was "a range of repressive attempts and initiatives that were frequently at cross purposes, with some in explicit contradiction with each other." He specifically identifies "three . . . distinct repressive approaches taken to Black street gangs in Chicago in the late 60s and early 70s"—the Rangers/Nation/Rukns in particular.[67] First, the city's Democratic machine, and therefore the local government and police, set out to destroy the gangs and preserve white dominance over the Black community—keeping the Democrats in charge of the government, white businessmen running the economy, and the Mafia in control of prostitution, drugs, and protection rackets.

This attempt at maintaining the local balance of power was in some ways at odds with the second strategy, incorporated through the OEO as a part of the Johnson administration's War on Poverty: "essentially hiring sections of the Black Gang leadership structure" to relieve the pressures that might otherwise fuel rebellion, and sometimes trying to use them, with FBI direction, as a counter-force against radicals. (Johnson's strategy was in turn opposed by congressional Republicans, who pushed for hearings to investigate the inevitable corruption and mismanagement that resulted.)

Third, some liberal South Side churches, in partnership with and under the guidance of a group of academic sociologists, encouraged the organization to reinvent itself as (in Hamerquist's terms) "a quasi-military formation with a 'charismatic' leadership and an authoritarian structure cloaked in the trappings of a religion"—in the process helping to legitimate the Rangers' takeover of local drug markets previously managed by the Mafia. The ultimate purpose, in Hamerquist's estimation, was "to develop the Black gang structure into a model for an alternative policing force for potentially rebellious populations."[68]

All three strategies treated the gang as a rival to the government. Mayor Richard Daley saw it as a competitor to be vanquished. The federal government, under Lyndon Johnson, sought to use the War on Poverty to co-opt the gang's leadership, neutralizing the group's rebellious potential while also opening it up to political manipulation. Most sophisticated was the sociologists' plan, which preserved the appearance of independence and even radicalism, while establishing the gang as a sort of paramilitary auxiliary, a semi-autonomous repressive force operating just outside of official society.[69]

Panthers and Rangers

All of this may be thought to make the Rangers rather dubious partners in the struggle for freedom.

But, seeking to expand on the success of the Rainbow Coalition, the Panthers' Fred Hampton approached the Rangers' Jeff Fort with a plan to unite all of Chicago's gangs. The idea was based on some earlier successes. In addition to the alliance with the Young Lords and the Young Patriots, a Panther chapter founded by former Disciples had already merged with Hampton's group.[70] And the Rangers, Vice Lords, and Egyptian Cobras all attended a "Free Huey" rally in October 1968 where one of the speakers described the various gangs as the "warriors we need" and urged unity.[71] A few weeks later, a coalition met to organize protests against the government's treatment of the Panthers; present at the meeting were representatives of the P Stone Nation, the Conservative Vice Lords, and other gangs, as well as more prominent figures like C. T. Vivian and Jesse Jackson.[72]

Hampton's proposal may also have been conceived of as a defensive measure, driven by necessity. When the Rainbow Coalition organized a march against police violence after the shooting of two Young Lords (one fatal), they found themselves being followed and threatened by a local Rangers affiliate, the Cobra Stones. One organizer, Hilda Ignatin, went to discuss the situation, and one of the Stones explained, "The police told us the Young Lords were helping the Panthers take over our projects." She managed to persuade them that that was untrue, that the police were lying and manipulating them, and the group joined the march—as did other gangs as the demonstration crossed through their turf.[73]

In January 1969, the Panthers and the Rangers finally met to discuss a possible partnership. It quickly became clear that they had very different arrangements in mind. Bobby Rush later recalled: "I think Jeff [Fort] was trying to recruit us into the Blackstone Rangers. . . . Our goal was to try to get Jeff more political. . . . We weren't trying to recruit the Stones into an apparatus. We wanted to build a coalition. I think they wanted us to become an affiliated organization."[74] The meeting ended without a clear resolution, but both sides agreed to keep talking and meet again. The follow-up meeting never took place, however.[75]

Merging the two groups would have doubled the size of the Panthers nationally.[76] The FBI naturally sought to prevent any alliance.[77] The Illinois field office suggested a rumor campaign that would lead Fort "to exact some form of retribution" against the BPP. They sent him an anonymous letter: "There's supposed to be a hit out for you."[78] This tactic was designed, as the FBI explained in a memo, "[to] intensify the degree of animosity between the two groups and occasion Fort to take retaliatory action which could disrupt the [BPP] or lead to reprisals against its leadership. Consideration has been given to a similar letter to the [BPP] alleging a Ranger plot against the [Panther] leadership; however, it is not felt this would be productive primarily because the [BPP] at present is not believed as violence prone as the Rangers to whom violent type activity—shooting and the like—is second nature."[79] The ploy failed. Fort was never inclined to believe the phony letter. In fact, he recognized it as a transparent attempt at manipulation and merely found it amusing.[80]

Eventually the police resorted to more direct measures. On the morning of December 4, 1969, at 4:00 a.m., fourteen police armed with submachine guns literally shot their way into Hampton's apartment. The police fired ninety-eight rounds, killing Fred Hampton and Mark Clark (head of the Peoria, Illinois, BPP) and injuring three others. Hampton was shot five times—three times in the chest and then twice in the head.[81]

Two thousand Stones made a brief but dramatic appearance at Fred Hampton's funeral.[82] And even after Hampton's death, Jeff Fort continued to dream of an alliance. In a 1970 editorial, he called for unity between the Panthers, Disciples, Vice Lords, and Rangers, writing: "The greatest and wildest dream of the fathers and mothers, men and women, sisters and brothers in the Black Chicago community is that we settle our differences and truly come together. Our unity is also the thing that [is] most feared [by] our oppressors. This is obvious from all the foul schemes our oppressors have used to keep us divided."[83]

The Entrepreneurial Spirit

In Sakai's assessment—weighing the cooperation with the police against the tentative overtures to the Panthers—"the Blackstone Rangers and the Disciples were never 'revolutionary,' or even usually militant." They were instead fundamentally cynical, opportunistic, and predatory: "The youth gang leadership openly and honestly looked to their own interests, bargaining and maneuvering with all sides to get the best 'deal.'"[84] Despite their rhetoric, the gangs displayed "an opposition to grass-roots Black organization," viewing civil rights groups as both a threat to the stability of their rackets and as rivals in competition for recruits and prestige. At the same time, "gang leaders had a strong natural orientation towards protecting white business in Woodlawn. They viewed the community—people and commerce and real estate—as a resource to be mined for its profitability. Every white businessman who left the area simply meant a source of potential income lost."[85]

That, of course, is the relationship implied by a protection racket.

Taking these facts together, Sakai concludes that "gang leaders had several important points of political unity with the government."[86] He attributes this alignment mainly to the "lumpenproletarian" class character of gang members. But we might find another explanation in the nature of the organizations themselves—both the gangs and the state.

Gangster States

Recognizing the shared orientation that Sakai outlines, one wonders if the issue of gang politics has been wrongly framed. Perhaps the relevant comparison is not between gangs and *insurgents* but between gangs and *states*.

The historian Charles Tilly, in his brief and penetrating essay "War Making and State Making as Organized Crime," argued that the projects of government and that of crime are essentially similar and that both can be fairly characterized as protection rackets.[87] Tilly doesn't say that gangs and governments are identical but that they "belong on the same continuum"—which implies difference and well as resemblance. "What distinguished the violence produced by states from the violence delivered by anyone else?," he asks rhetorically, and then replies: "In the long run, enough to make the division between 'legitimate' and 'illegitimate' force credible. Eventually, the personnel of states purveyed violence on a larger scale, more effectively, more efficiently, with wider assent from their subject populations, and with readier collaboration from neighboring authorities than did the personnel of other organizations."[88] The main differences, in other words, are those of scale, power, public assent, and peer recognition.[89]

By this telling, which Tilly backs with historical accounts of the formation of European nation-states as well as clear-sighted conceptual analysis, governments are just extremely successful criminal enterprises. States are built by crooks who have managed to accumulate enough power that they can eliminate their rivals, impose peace by monopolizing violence, and in the process win a measure of popular support.[90]

The economists Stergios Skaperdas and Constantinos Syropoulos begin at the other end of the spectrum and reach similar conclusions. Given the shared tendency to control territory and exclude rivals, "it could be useful to think of organizations like gangs as states."[91] They outline the process as follows: "When force determines how many resources you can receive and the amount of force you exert depends on your resources, there are compounding rewards to having an initial superiority in resources." Therefore, also, there are compounding rewards when it comes to monopolizing force. The type of organization emerging from this competitive struggle will most probably be "subjugational, authoritarian and hierarchical." However, the "rulers would always want to reduce the waste of resources associated with the use of force and protracted conflict if it could be done with minimal threat to their rule. One way to do that would be [to] convince their subjects of their rule's legitimacy."[92]

Legitimate Force

The relationship between legitimacy and violence is necessarily a complex one. Legitimacy simultaneously makes violence more available and constrains its use. When an agency's violence is widely viewed as legitimate, it is less likely to provoke resistance, but the very need to maintain the appearance of legitimacy means that, on the whole, such violence must be kept within socially prescribed bounds.[93] Fortunately, legitimacy may also make violence less *necessary* as it brings access to other resources and broadens the range of available strategies and tactics. Individuals, institutions, and movements that have achieved a measure of legitimacy are more likely—whether or not they invoke coercive sanctions like violence—to have their claims respected, their instructions obeyed, their interests protected.[94] Violence may still be used, sometimes in large measure, but legitimacy reduces the *dependence* on force. In fact, an overreliance on coercion is one indication that legitimacy is lacking.[95]

Necessarily, then, legitimacy cannot be understood as the property of the state, in either sense—as a rightful possession or as an essential characteristic. Legitimacy, instead, emerges as part of an ongoing social process, typically a political struggle. As such, it is continuously being produced and always being tested and contested.

Insurgencies arise where the state's legitimacy is weak and, though rebellions fail for any number of reasons, when they succeed it is in large part because the insurgent forces have gained the support and loyalty of the population. The political is primary, in two senses. It defines the cause of the conflict, and it often determines the outcome.[96]

The threat posed by groups like the Panthers was less in their potential for violence than in their challenge to the legitimacy of the state. (That explains, among other things, why the FBI specifically targeted the Panthers' free breakfast program; it anchored them in the community and bought them broad support.)[97] States, in other words, would rather face gangs than insurgencies; they prefer crime to revolution.

Part Three: After Insurgency

Decimation and Degeneration

Gang violence decreased during the Black Power era.[98] But the defeat of the Panthers triggered a subsequent drift into a new kind of gangsterism, epitomized by the rise of the Crips and then, shortly after, the Bloods.[99] Mike Davis explains: "[The] decimation of the Panthers led directly to a recrudescence of gangs in the early 1970s. . . . The Crips, however perversely, inherited the Panther aura of fearlessness and transmitted the ideology of armed vanguardism . . . [albeit] shorn of its program."[100]

As the Crips set about aggressively expanding their territory, their smaller, neighborhood-based rivals began to affiliate in a defensive alliance under the banner of the Bloods. With these two supergangs competing for the same territory—and control of the associated markets—all the factors necessary for decades of fratricidal warfare fell into place. Under the counterinsurgency model, that result was predictable and even desirable. The U.S. Army's *Counterinsurgency* field manual (FM 3-24) states frankly: "Throughout history, many insurgencies have degenerated into criminality. This occurred as the primary movements disintegrated and the remaining elements were cast adrift. *Such disintegration is desirable; it replaces a dangerous, ideologically inspired body of disaffiliated individuals with a less dangerous but more diverse body, normally of very uneven character.*"[101]

The Sterner Stuff of Politics

The same degeneration is evident in the decline of the Black Panther Party itself.

In the 1970s, Panther founder and minister of defense Huey P. Newton turned toward gangsterism, partly to feed his own cocaine habit. Surrounded by unquestioning loyalists and often intoxicated, he began to lose his grip on reality. As a result, Bloom and Martin report, "the Oakland Black Panther Party became increasingly cultish, resembling a social service organization, motivated by revolutionary ideology, with a mafioso bent."[102]

In 1972, Newton formed a security force called simply "the squad." Answerable only to Newton himself, its members were initially responsible for security and internal discipline, but their mandate soon expanded.[103] Former Panther Flores Forbes later recalled, "We created a special unit that would protect our leaders and do other kinds of activities related to what Huey Newton called the sterner stuff of politics."[104] Under Newton's orders, special security squads started shaking down drug dealers, pimps, and after-hours clubs.[105] As Forbes admits, "We were going to take over the underworld."[106] George Robinson, one of Huey's bodyguards, explained the plan for speakeasies and after-hours clubs: "What Huey wanted was for everybody who ran an establishment to give part of their earnings to the breakfast program, the school, or the other programs we had going in the community. Huey demanded that, and, of course, there was resistance there for a minute until they found out they were in the wrong league. . . . The people in the speakeasies knew who Huey was, and some people genuinely liked and respected him, while others were afraid of him. It was as simple as that."[107]

In Oakland, the Panthers had previously engaged in small-time drug dealing and gambling operations to fund their work.[108] And they had always tried to get pimps and drug dealers to donate to the survival programs.[109] Prior to his political career, Huey Newton himself had been a minor thief, fence, quick change artist, and (briefly) a pimp—"a minor criminal," in the words of his friend and later BPP chief of staff David Hilliard.[110] Newton—who viewed crime simply as "illegitimate capitalism"—had long expressed a desire "to transform many of the so-called criminal actions going on in the streets into something political."[111] Hilliard elaborated: "Our thrust was to organize an illegitimate economic resource, connect it to our community programs, and put the money into our programs, with the end result being more respect for a segment of the community that had been historically criticized as a pariah."[112] Crime could bring money (and, though Hilliard does not say it, muscle) into the party, and the cachet of the party could lend a sense of prestige and respectability to the pimps and drug dealers who contributed to the cause. The problem, of course, is that it soon became hard to tell which was the ends and which was the means. Who was transforming whom? Was the party politicizing the criminal element, or were the criminals corrupting the party?[113]

Radicals like Geronimo Pratt ceased to regard Newton's faction as a political organization at all and took to calling them the "Peralta street gang."[114] The FBI likewise saw the embrace of organized crime as the terminal phase of the party's decline. An agent reported in one memo: "The Black Panther party (BPP) is a thing of the past. . . . Newton is now attempting to create an organization . . . to control among many things, dope pushers, prostitutes, and private social clubs. . . . Newton has, to date, been very success-ful in creating a 'family' type organization under which he rules."[115]

Eventually, the story reached its tragic denouement. On August 23, 1989, Huey Newton, founder and leader of the Black Panther Party, was killed by a crack dealer, probably during an attempted robbery.[116]

Crime and Legitimacy

Tarnishing the Black Panther Party's reputation by associating it with criminality was a deliberate repressive tactic, one to which the group's indiscipline left it vulnerable. As historian Judson Jeffries sees it, "When news reports told of Panthers being arrested for threatening a small business owner, warring with other Black groups, or torturing and murdering suspected Panther informants, understandably a segment of the public began to view the Panthers as little more than small-time gangsters."[117]

The dangers here were real, not merely as a matter of public perception. Indeed, the potential for a criminal drift exists in-herently within any revolutionary movement. Bloom and Martin explain: "In noninsurgent organizations, established laws and cus-toms are assumed and largely respected. . . . Within insurgent orga-nizations like the Black Panther Party, law and custom are viewed as oppressive and illegitimate. . . . As a result, defining acceptable types of transgressions of law and custom, and maintaining disci-pline within these constraints often poses a serious challenge."[118]

At their best, the Panthers were sensitive to this problem. Especially at the end, however, a series of internal faults made them less and less capable of addressing it. In his paper "Explaining the Demise of the Black Panther Party: The Role of Internal Factors," Ollie A. Johnson III, points to three problems: "(1) in-tra-party conflict, (2) strategic organizational mistakes, and (3) a new authoritarianism."[119] More specifically, he identifies these as the Newton-Cleaver faction fight, which ultimately split the orga-nization; the shift to electoral politics in the Oakland branch; and

Newton's post-prison leadership style, involving personal abuse, individual control of party funds, centralized power, and the move to organized crime.[120]

It is with the scars of hard experience that Lorenzo Komboa Ervin—a former gang member, then Panther, who later turned toward anarchism—advises those looking to continue the legacy of the Panthers, to "Reject Militarism," "Reject Vanguardism," and "Reject Personality Cult[s]." Instead, he urges, "Build a Mass Movement," and especially, "Build a Movement with a More Libertarian Structure and Ideology."[121]

To the degree that insurgent groups think of themselves as aspiring states, adopting a party form and military structure, it is likely that in the period of their decline, they will degenerate toward gangsterism. Conversely, to the degree that they pattern their organizing on that of the street gang, it is likely that as they achieve power they will replicate the coercive and repressive features of a state. This observation says less about insurgencies as such than about the close resemblance between gangs and states. And it suggests that insurgent movements, to fulfill their liberatory potential, must find and follow a different logic, must move along a different axis—not seizing power but dispersing it, not trying to monopolize force but to generalize freedom.

Considerations

I began this essay by considering the threat gang alliances pose to the police and what the police response—specifically, the domestic application of counterinsurgency warfare—tells us about how the state understands that threat. I considered a few examples of gangs involving themselves in politics, the difficulties they experience in making that transition, and the problem this poses for any theoretical treatment of gangs as insurgents. What I offer instead is a conceptualization of gangs as nascent states, borrowing largely from

Charles Tilly's analysis of the state as organized crime. That analysis is particularly striking because it concerns activities—governing and crime—which are generally considered as opposites.[122] By placing them on a continuum, however, we can see how much "crime" remains in the process of governing, and how much "governing" is involved in organized crime. So too can we see how both "government" and "crime" may represent permanent temptations—and fatal diversions—for movements seeking radical social change.

With this discussion in mind, the logic of using counterinsurgency to combat gangs becomes clear. It is not that gangs *are* insurgents but that the authorities wish to prevent them from *becoming* insurgents. At the same time, governments are only too happy to see insurgencies disintegrate into rival gangs.

It is a truism that states monopolize rather than eliminate violence. What is less commonly recognized is an important qualifier; as one RAND Corporation report on counterinsurgency explains: "The key in COIN is not to monopolize force but to monopolize legitimate force."[123] A government can tolerate, and even exploit, the persistence of violence outside of its control—as long as that violence is widely regarded as illegitimate. One way that the state enforces its monopoly is by criminalizing its rivals. It can then legitimize its own violence by framing it as protection against their violence.[124] Public fear of illegal violence—whether crime or terrorism—can bolster support for the state's repressive apparatus, the curtailment of individual rights, and the intensification of state violence against suspect populations. For states, then, violence is not the problem—not even illegal violence. The crucial question is that of legitimacy.

Both gangs and insurgencies are rivals to the state, but not all rivals are equal. From the state's point of view, gangs are preferable to guerrillas. As gangs come to resemble insurgents, they become more dangerous to the state, even if they become less dangerous to the public. Because legitimacy is ultimately more important than force, the political threat is more dangerous than the criminal one.

Contrarily, as insurgencies decay and become more gang-like, they become less dangerous to the state but very likely more dangerous to the community.

Gangs and states each offer a kind of protection, but in each case the price for the client population is a relationship of dependency and exploitation. When insurgencies aspire to state power—or, less ambitiously, to the armed control of territory within an existing state—they will generally tend to replicate these same dynamics. The challenge for liberatory movements, then, is not merely to launch an insurgency capable of overturning the existing power structure but to create new ways of relating, of organizing, of exercising and sharing power, that do not themselves reproduce the logic of a protection racket.

Street Fights, Gang Wars, and Insurrections

Proud Boys versus Antifa (versus Police)

Part One: From Street Fights to Insurrection

Altercations

On January 6, 2021, a crowd of thousands of Trump loyalists surged through police lines and occupied the U.S. Capitol in an attempt to disrupt the certification of the election results establishing Joe Biden as the forty-sixth president.[1] More than 140 people were injured in the attack. Four died, though only one from direct violence—Ashli Babbitt, shot by Capitol Police as she tried to force her way into the House Chamber.[2]

It is too early to tell whether January 6 will be seen as the opening act in a new drama of rightwing insurgency or as the pathetic final scene of an absurdist play, one that ends with the cast urging the audience to tear apart the theater. Either way, it came after years of dress rehearsals. In the preceding months, armed groups had attacked state capitols in Michigan, Idaho, Georgia, Oregon, and Virginia.[3] Throughout the summer of 2020, militia groups had stood guard to defend businesses from looters amid the nationwide unrest sparked by the Minneapolis police murder of George Floyd, an unarmed Black man.[4] Later, impromptu posses mustered with arms to protect small towns from "Antifa busses" shipping in rioters from the big city. The rumors were baseless: there was no black bloc bus tour.[5] But the experience laid the groundwork for later anti-Antifa patrols. Convinced that antifascists had started the wildfires then engulfing the western states, in September armed groups set up roadblocks, intended to deter arsonists and looters but only impeding evacuation and intimidating journalists—especially people of color.[6]

All of that occurred, of course, in the shadow of Charlottesville.

In 2017, a proposal to remove Confederate statues from a Virginia college town had provided the pretext for a vast "Unite the Right" rally. Neo-nazis carried oddly kitschy tiki torches and chanted "Jews will not replace us!" Fascist demonstrators and antifascist counterdemonstrators brawled in the streets for hours. James Alex Fields, a man associated with the far-right Vanguard America (since rebranded as the Patriot Front), purposefully crashed his car into a crowd of leftwing counterprotesters, killing a young woman named Heather Heyer and injuring nineteen others.[7] Rather than uniting the right, the events of that day fragmented the movement, as notable figures tried desperately (and unconvincingly) to distance themselves from the bloodshed. Blame was cast in all directions.[8]

Charlottesville—and the murder of Heyer above all—got the public's attention, raising the alarm about a budding fascist threat and generating sympathy for antifascist protesters.[9] (Most notably, after a group of black bloc anarchists formed a barrier between hostile rightwingers and antiracist clergy, Cornel West credited them with saving his life.)[10] But the day's events proved less decisive than antifascist observers initially hoped.[11] The fascist right, though politically defeated, enjoyed a renewed sense of significance, feeling the potential of its surprising numbers and finding a new taste for street fighting.[12] There was, additionally, a tantalizing flirtation with power at the very top of government. In the first of many similar equivocations, President Trump condemned violence "on many sides," refusing to single out white supremacists for blame.[13]

The next several years would see a whole series of mini-"Charlottesvilles," street clashes between rightwing and leftwing demonstrators. In the typical case, a far-right group would announce a rally in a famously liberal city like Berkeley or Portland. Ostensibly it would address some issue like immigration, gun rights, or free speech, but the real point was simple provocation.[14] As Southern Poverty Law Center senior research analyst Cassie Miller explains, "Each time, the goal of these events has been the same: to incite violent confrontations with counter-protesters, blame any resulting violence on the left, and press for further repression and retaliation against those they consider their political adversaries."[15] The result was an atmosphere that one anarchist characterized as "Weimar without the art."[16]

Adversaries

Two groups emerged as consistent antagonists in these conflicts: Proud Boys and Antifa.

What exactly these groups are and how best to describe them is a matter of perpetual controversy. The Proud Boys call themselves a "pro-Western fraternity," but that only raises further questions, as both of those words are open to interpretation.[17] Their critics often call them white supremacists, but that on its own is hardly more clear and even a bit confusing, given their multiracial membership and explicit disavowal of racism. What we can say with certainty is that it is an all-male organization, with a vague but clearly far-right ideology, and that it has eagerly engaged in violent clashes against leftists, often fighting alongside open racists.[18]

If it is hard to sum up the Proud Boys in a phrase, it is both far harder and far easier to characterize Antifa. The Proud Boys are at least an organization, with a single founder, identifiable leadership, and official publications. Antifa has none of those things. It is, as FBI director Chris Wray put it, "more of an ideology or a movement than an organization."[19] At least it is not a *single* organization but something more like an idea that can be replicated by any number of small groups without any central coordination. In a way the idea is simple: *Antifa* is just a contraction of *antifascist*. But the very simplicity allows for a great deal of diversity. Politics, strategies, and tactics may vary widely between groups. Complicating things further is the obvious fact that not everyone who is against fascism is Antifa. Antifa is the militant edge to a much broader antifascist consensus that includes liberals and mainstream conservatives as well as the street-fighting radicals. Sociologist Stanislav Vysotsky points out that most of the work done by Antifa groups is nonviolent, involving "information gathering, educational efforts, and cultural work" in addition to "public pressure campaigns and public shaming." However: "Ultimately, it is the willingness to use force in confrontations with fascists that delineates antifa activism."[20]

The Proud Boys and Antifa stand as virtual opposites, not only in terms of right and left and racist and antiracist, but also in the very different routes they have traveled on their way to the riot. Though its ancestry is complex, featuring many and diverse forebears, Antifa is heir to a tradition epitomized by an earlier organization, Anti-Racist Action, which in turn evolved from a skinhead street gang, the Baldies. Put differently: a street gang became politicized, developed into a different kind of organization, and multiple iterations later, the movement still finds its politics and culture shaped by that lineage. The Proud Boys, in contrast, were drawn together by ideology and quickly formed into a political organization with pronounced gang tendencies. These two stories move along opposite trajectories. In one, a gang is thrust into a political conflict and is transformed. In the other, a particular set of politics crystallizes in the form of a gang and then propels it to violent action.

While not offering anything like complete histories, in what follows I hope to trace a specific throughline, concentrating on the gang-like elements of each group and considering the implications for radical political action. I begin in England, with the skinheads.

Part Two: Skinhead Wars and After

White Youth, Black Youth

In genealogical terms, the skinhead subculture stands as a practical refutation of nazi ideology. Originating in late-sixties England, it emerged as a self-consciously working-class variant at the intersection of the mod and rude boy subcultures. As both a development from and reaction against the mods of the early sixties, "hard mods" did away with the dandified dress, preferring instead a stereotyped working-class uniform of close-cropped hair, blue jeans, and boots.[21] Soon after, they adopted elements of the culture of the young Jamaican "rude boys," both the dress and the music—sharp suits and pork pie hats, ska and rocksteady. Both groups cultivated a persona of criminality and a reputation for violence, sometimes casual and sometimes organized along gang lines. As the two subcultures drew closer together they produced something new.[22]

That initial phase was short-lived, but the skinhead subculture was reinvigorated and reimagined a few years later in a new context created by punk rock. The look changed, especially after it migrated to the United States: bomber jackets, camo pants, taller boots, and even shorter hair. Purists were disdainful of the newer version, dismissing its adherents as being merely "bald punks" or, worse, "boneheads." These fashion choices were soon politicized, as the newer skins moved to the right, and the originalists, in response, became not merely non-racist but explicitly *anti*racist.[23]

There were certainly elements of the culture that lent themselves to rightwing co-optation, especially its cult of masculinity and a readiness for violence.[24] These tendencies were particularly potent, cultural critics Stephen Duncombe and Maxwell Tremblay note, when combined with "punk's sense of victimization, its valorization of oppositional solidarity, its creativity and mobilization of DIY cultural networks, its understanding of the desire for the forbidden and the shocking, and the simple raw emotionality and anger of its expression."[25] Punk's need to shock, its love of giving offense, its continuous flirting with taboos, opened the door to extremism of all types—political as well as aesthetic, right as much as left. Ironic swastikas too easily made way for real swastikas.

By the late seventies, the British Movement, the British National Party, and the National Front were actively recruiting skinheads, happy to channel their aggressive energies toward attacking immigrants, gays, and the left.[26] In addition to the allure of street fighting, fascism promised to restore at a national level just the sort of traditional (if imagined) community the skins sought to reproduce in a subcultural microcosm. "The skinhead style," John Clarke explains, "represents an attempt to re-create through the 'mob' [read: *gang*] the traditional working-class community, as a substitution for the *real* decline of the latter."[27] As one skinhead told an interviewer, "It's a community, a gang, isn't it? It's only another word for community. Kids, thugs, whatever."[28]

WAR Boys

The shift to the right only accelerated as skinhead style migrated overseas, and the American punk scene was soon overrun by racist goons.[29]

Seeing an opportunity and inspired by the National Front's gains in the UK, Tom Metzger, the leader of the White Aryan Resistance, sought to recruit skinheads as foot soldiers in a race war.[30] The Southern California WARskins represented an early effort to bring this about, but the name proved divisive and struck other boneheads as presumptuous. Clark Martell, founder of the Chicago Area Skinheads (CASH), met with somewhat more success bringing midwestern skinhead crews into WAR.[31] But as antifascist scholar Shane Burley notes, "What came out of these skinheads was more a gang culture than a seasoned political organization. . . . This led to a culture of seemingly random violence, where most political acts were spontaneous and as bloody as they were disorganized."[32] Portland's East Side White Pride, for example, was hardly what could be called an activist organization: its political ambitions seem to have been limited to distributing racist propaganda and drunkenly attacking random queers or people of color—or, if none were available, whomever happened by.[33]

The results were often deadly: between 1987 and 1993, white power skinheads killed at least twenty-eight people nationwide.[34] As the nazis became more bold and their violence escalated, other skinheads resolved to stop them.

Righteous Violence

In Minneapolis, a multiracial skinhead crew called the Baldies began fighting nazis by necessity.[35]

"The Baldies started out as just a bunch of friends liking the skinhead culture," one of their founding members, Jay Nevilles ("Gator"), recalls. "Our plan wasn't to be antifascist or antiracist, we just wanted to have a skinhead crew."[36] But they found themselves facing another crew, a group called the White Knights, led by a Klan organizer, sporting nazi insignia, and known for attacking Blacks, gays, and homeless people.[37] The White Knights were a threat that the Baldies could not ignore. Mic Crenshaw, another of the original Baldies, explains, "We felt a moral obligation to meet violence with violence."[38]

Though the Baldies weren't afraid of a fight, they didn't *start* by fighting. "We started by talking with some of the younger people involved with the Nazis," Kieran Knutson says, "making sure they knew what they will be defending if there is a fight."[39] Those conversations "gave people a chance to think about their decisions."[40] They "let them know that [their stance] carried consequences . . . it gave them fair warning."[41] (Pointedly: "The next time we see you, if you're still a White Knight, then you're going to get your ass whooped.")[42] Some who got that warning took the opportunity to change their ways.[43] Some even joined the Baldies—"an outcome," historian Mark Bray notes, "that would have been far less likely had they been attacked immediately."[44]

Still, the threat of a beating—the Baldies called it "righteous violence"—was essential, and sometimes the threat had to be made good.[45] The important thing was to keep up the pressure, without relent. "After a while, every time we saw them we confronted them," Knutson says.[46] The strategy worked: in the summer of 1987, the White Knights disbanded.[47]

Crucially too, the Baldies weren't fighting alone. First they approached others in the scene: skinheads, punks, skaters, anarchists. But they soon looked further, especially to ethnic gangs. "The Black, Latino gangs, people in Native American community and their street organizations," Mic Crenshaw explains; basically anyone who "would take a stand fighting against these white power skinheads."[48] So when the Baldies read in *Maximumrocknroll* about the problems people were having elsewhere, they wrote to kids in other cities.[49] Some went on tour with the band Blind Approach and met with other skinheads, including Brew City Skins (from Milwaukee) and SHOC (Skinheads of Chicago).[50]

In city after city, the story was much the same. One activist from Cincinnati pointed to "a place called Short Vine, which is a short strip where there were tattoo parlors, . . . record stores, clubs, and bars. This strip was our life. Our life involved two and a half blocks. . . . This was *our* space that we had to defend from nazis. And that's the *beginning* of this. It wasn't this view of fascism in Europe and its creeping into the United States; it was literally defending this space from nazis."[51] But as they made contact with other groups, "it became bigger than two and a half blocks. . . . It allowed us to connect to a movement that was bigger than just the scene, just the music."[52]

Jabari, from SHOC, credits the Baldies for politicizing what could have just remained scene drama. He told Mic Crenshaw and others involved in the podcast *It Did Happen Here*: "Up to that point, we just liked to brawl, we liked to fight in the streets, that was it. While we believed it had some philosophical underpinnings, when it comes down to it, we were just fighting and drinking. But then when y'all gave us the language of antiracist action, direct action, and confrontation and principled antifascism, it's like, ahh . . . here we go. That's what we were missing. That was the missing component."[53]

In January 1989, over a hundred skinheads from cities throughout the Midwest came to Minneapolis for the Martin Luther King Day weekend. They had a meeting in the public library branch in Uptown, and afterward marched through the city spray-painting over racist graffiti. From this meeting, crews from around the Midwest joined together to form the Syndicate.[54] As Crenshaw explains: "The Syndicate was basically this network of anti-racist skinhead crews and anti-fascist crews that were ready to hunt down Nazis in their cities because we understood that in order to confront violent racists, we couldn't just do it ideologically and we couldn't do it with words and language. We could do all those things and we were doing all those things, but we had to be willing to find them where they were and fight them. That was the beginning of that culture."[55]

Of course the Baldies did not invent fighting nazis. And, facing the same sorts of opponents in similar contexts, it is hardly surprising that skinhead crews in various cities reacted in much the same fashion and used existing subculture networks to organize regionally. The Baldies' specific contribution was to reach outside of the subculture and build a lasting, national organization. If it had not been them, it likely would have been somebody else.

From reading British anarchist publications like *Class War* and *Black Flag*, the Baldies learned about Anti-Fascist Action, a British coalition formed in 1985, with participation from the Jewish Socialists' Group, the Class War Federation, the Direct Action Movement, *Searchlight* magazine, Red Action (formerly the Anti-Nazi League), and number smaller local groups.[56] Taking this as inspiration, in 1987 the Baldies founded a formal organization, Anti-Racist Action (ARA)—*not* "Anti-Fascist Action," because they felt that "fascism" was unfamiliar in an American context—and they started pursuing alliances outside of the skinhead scene, on more of a political basis.[57]

It took some time to break out of the subcultural ghetto, and the success was always somewhat mixed.[58] But by 1992, Chicago ARA's Marty Williams recounts, "ARA had evolved from a primarily skinhead-based crew to a national organization in many cities, attracting students, workers, anarchist punks, and older, more established leftwing activists."[59] Perhaps more impressive, by the mid-nineties, ARA had extended beyond the cities and had chapters in small towns throughout the Midwest.[60]

Counterculture, Counter-Recruitment

Even as they were reaching beyond the world of skinhead and punk, "A central element of the overall ARA approach," one member wrote, was always "the cultivation of an anti-racist/anti-fascist counterculture. This has proceeded primarily through the organizing of regular Rock Against Racism concerts and also weekend parties, as well as the creation of an ARA 'style.'" This emphasis developed from that first effort to take the scene back from the boneheads, but it also constituted a strategy for counter-recruitment, making the left more appealing than the right but on the same terms: "Few young people are attracted to fascist organizations on the basis of ideology alone. Most are attracted to the cultural scene first, through the music, parties, or friends and only later drawn into the movement and its ideas. Rather than ignore this reality, ARA has actively sought to promote a compelling, vibrant, and fun culture of resistance to attract young people and provide an alternative to the nazis."[61]

Ironically, the group's *success* in turning racists into antiracists—whether through the threat of violence or with "positive peer pressure"—was sometimes cited by critics as evincing shallow politics and a lack of commitment.[62] The Southern Poverty Law Center (SPLC), paraphrasing sociologist Kathleen Blee, wrote dismissively in "Roots of the ARA": "Ideology and politics had little to do with the conflict for most of the warring skins. They were like street gang members, lost and lonely youth, attracted to the excitement, the violence, the sound of sirens, the sight of blood. . . . Which side someone belonged to often depended on who their friends were or the parties they attended."[63] That may well be true, but to frame it as a criticism misses the point: ARA wasn't trying to save souls but to destroy the white power movement. Drawing the fascists' base away from them was one strategy for doing so.[64] Viewed that way, *why* someone lined up against the nazis was less important than *that* they did.

There was, likewise, "a lot of tension about our racial composition as an anti-racist group," one member of Cincinnati ARA admits. "It was overwhelmingly white." Partly this was an accident of the group's history: "We came out of the white punk scene, an overwhelmingly white punk scene." But it also reflected something of their overall strategy: "Where we were coming from, we were in competition with these Klanspeople. . . . So the idea of recruiting white people is *exactly* what we wanted to do. We wanted to recruit white people away from the racists."[65]

Sometimes they did. And sometimes, as the SPLC notes, recruiting had more to do with social circumstance and personal connection than with careful deliberation and political principle. For individual skinheads, their allegiance might be determined simply by which side approached them first, the attractions—a sense of purpose and belonging, a way to prove yourself—being largely the same.[66] But what begins as a chance meeting can develop into friendship and personal loyalty, and then into political engagement and a deeper sense of commitment. (This is how a lot of organizing works.)[67] So some of those wayward youth, who could have ended up on either side, chose a team—or that team chose them—and they grew into stalwarts for the cause. Alex Stuck, a member of the Hoosier Anti-Racist Movement (HARM), was one. "I wasn't sure if I was racist or anti-racist. . . . I just knew I was pissed off," he says, looking back. "I was a disenfranchised white youth . . . and thank God they [HARM] got to me first. I could have easily went the opposite direction."[68]

ARA's cultural work—specifically, its roots in the skinhead scene—was absolutely critical but equally limiting. "The success of ARA could be found in its being a truly organic product of a youth culture," Rory McGowan later wrote. "[But] larger political concerns became subordinate to the internal scene life."[69] In addition to being overwhelmingly white, ARA was almost exclusively a youth movement. "If you were twenty-five, you were old," one member remembers.[70] It was also very much a boys' club—"a macho male dominated scene"—as some of its members admitted at the time.[71] All of this, of course, pointed back to the group's skinhead origins. As much as the shared culture and social ties were a strength, the persistent subcultural elements were also a source of frustration. "One of the distinct weaknesses," in the view of a former member from Cincinnati, was that ARA "could never get out of being . . . largely one subculture."[72]

Still, whatever its limitations, the organization's reach was impressive. By 1997, Anti-Racist Action had almost two hundred chapters and around two thousand members.[73] Its newsletter went to twenty-five thousand addresses and was likely read by many times that number of people.[74] The strength of the organization lay in its scale and the sense of connection.

"Each scene, on our own, we were nothing," one member said. "We get together, we're ARA."[75]

The Battle for Portland

In 1989 and 1990, both the Minneapolis Baldies and Chicago ARA sent organizers to Portland, Oregon, a city embroiled in its own skinhead wars.[76] In 1988, Portland had achieved national notoriety when a nazi gang beat an Ethiopian immigrant to death with a baseball bat. Three members of East Side White Pride—Ken Mieske, Kyle Brewster, and Steve Strasser—went to prison for the murder of Mulugeta Seraw.

It was hardly the first serious incident—not even the first murder—and less dramatic violence was ubiquitous.[77] M. Treloar, an organizer with the Coalition for Human Dignity, later recalled, "There were daytime attacks on people of color in Pioneer Courthouse Square and 'hippies' along Hawthorne Avenue [Hawthorne Boulevard] by small gangs of nazi punks. Weekend beer bashes with scores of boneheads were a common event, with physical attacks and racist graffiti sprees a common aftermath."[78] But Mulugeta Seraw's murder was a turning point. "The decision was finally made to attack the boneheads where they lived, worked and played," Treloar said.[79]

The first stand was made, as one participant recalls, at a punk show where "everybody showed up with bats and stood out front." The boneheads circled the area in cars, sometimes jumping out to attack people on side streets. But aside from "probably a couple scuffles," there was no major confrontation. The nazis didn't like the odds, and they left. "That happened for three shows in a row and then they, for quite a while, they just quit coming." But the problem wasn't limited to the punk scene. "We decided that it wasn't enough to protect the shows, people at those shows. We wanted to push further."[80]

Tactics ranged from intelligence-gathering, to sabotaging the nazis' vehicles ("a bunch of Jolly Ranchers . . . in the gas tanks"), to posting fliers in their neighborhoods and picketing their workplaces.[81] "It may have been a shit job," Treloar boasted, "but in every case where we placed a picket, the bonehead lost the shit job, usually that day and usually because his co-workers refused to work while he was there." More important than "be[ing] confronted when they appeared publicly," Treloar thought, was the fact that the fascists were "attacked in ways they were not prepared for."[82]

Unity

It wasn't all street fights and parties. Aside from their signature confrontations with boneheads, across the country ARA took on a variety of political projects, including the defense of abortion clinics, Palestinian solidarity work, and political prisoner support.[83] Minneapolis ARA organized a same-sex kiss-in outside a meeting of religious right groups.[84] In the mid-nineties, as a way of "attacking more institutionalized racism," several chapters took up copwatching—the systematic observation of police on the streets with an eye to documenting (and thus discouraging) misconduct.[85]

As they expanded their focus, ARA continued to build alliances with groups like the Center for Democratic Renewal (formerly the Anti-Klan Network), People Against Racist Terror, the Sojourner Truth Organization, the Love and Rage Revolutionary Anarchist Federation, the October League, and the John Brown Anti-Klan Committee.[86] Toronto ARA worked with the Ontario Coalition Against Poverty and the Black Action Defense Committee.[87] Minneapolis ARA worked with a student group to paint over racist graffiti.[88] Portland ARA partnered with the Coalition for Human Dignity, Radical Women, and the Lesbian Community Project and organized benefit shows for the Leonard Peltier support committee and a domestic violence shelter. ("Raised a few bucks and then got raided by the cops," one member recalls.)[89] In Detroit, ARA supported striking newspaper workers and students who staged a walkout in protest of conditions in the schools, and the chapter tried to connect the two struggles.[90]

ARA's activities, along with the size and militancy of the chapters, might vary by location, but there were clear principles that provided a sense of connection.[91] Their Points of Unity read:

1. We go where they go: Wherever fascists are organizing or active in public, we're there. . . . Never let the Nazis have the streets!

2. We don't rely on the cops or the courts to do our work for us. . . .

3. Non-sectarian defense of other antifascists: . . . We don't agree about everything and we have the right to differ openly. But in this movement an attack on one is an attack on us all. We stand behind each other.

4. We support abortion rights and reproductive freedom: ARA intends to do the hard work necessary to build a broad, strong movement against racism, sexism, anti-Semitism, homophobia, discrimination against the disabled, the oldest, the youngest and the most oppressed people. We intend to win![92]

Sharp Differences

There were some who had reservations about the ARA approach, even within the skinhead scene where the organization was initially strongest. Some more traditional skinheads saw ARA as "too political."[93] Sometimes that meant the skins were suspicious of the intentions of left-wing organizations.[94] Sometimes it meant they resented the "politically correct" culture of the left (e.g., "too many rules").[95] And sometimes it just meant too many meetings and not enough fighting: "You know, like doing security for marches is cool, doing protests outside of homes and businesses where Nazis are working's cool, but like, I wanted to just beat 'em up."[96]

This more raw approach developed into a different sort of organization. Skinheads Against Racial Prejudice (SHARP) was founded by Marcus Pacheco in New York in 1986, and the idea spread in large part thanks to the influence of Roddy Moreno's Oi Records.[97] But many antiracist skins, including some in and around SHARP, were deeply nationalistic and violently homophobic.[98] In New York, some antiracist but rightwing skinheads launched violent attacks against anarchists and routinely beat up gay men.[99] Most notably, in 1990 a member of the DMS crew (Doc Marten Skinheads), along with two of his friends, murdered a gay man name Julio Rivera, striking him ten times with the claw end of a hammer and stabbing him in the back.[100] Rejecting these right-wing, antigay, anticommunist politics, the May Day Crew split from SHARP and formed RASH (Red and Anarchist Skinheads). While never achieving the same prominence as SHARP, RASH became an international organization as well.[101]

In Portland, meanwhile, "For a hot minute, SHARP and ARA were synonymous," Mic Crenshaw says. "But as 1990 rolled into 1991, SHARPs emerged as a unique identity. . . . SHARP was loose. . . . SHARPs had few rules regarding conduct, and they didn't have regular meetings." One member described SHARP's attitude as "we're 2 Tone [blending ska and punk], we're working class, we're not dealing with your Nazi BS. And if you look at me sideways, I get to punch you in the face." He went on: "I can tell you that the people I hung out with, if you brought some nazi BS to me or the crew that I ran with, or the people that we hung around with, you might get your face cut off with a broken pint glass, you might end up getting your head stomped in by ten guys. You definitely were going to get something broken."[102]

The police and the press regularly dismissed SHARP as a gang, but really they may not have been even that well organized.[103] Apart from a post office box in New York, SHARP was not so much an organization as a moniker that anyone could adopt.[104] The Portland Police Bureau's Loren Christensen, a gang-squad detective and resident "expert" on skinhead violence, admitted as much. Though he listed both ARA and SHARP as gangs, he noted that the latter was "almost a generic term for antiracist skinheads."[105]

The energy that had been released by Portland's mix of ARA, SHARP, the Coalition of Human Dignity, and related organizations soon dissipated. By the mid-nineties, no one group predominated, and the next few years saw a proliferation of antiracist skinhead crews: SCAR (Skinheads Committed Against Racism), PUB (Portland United Boot Boys), the Rose City Bovver Boys, Intensified, and a local group taking on the name of the Baldies.[106]

Jason, an ARA organizer, describes the shift: "The energy

changed and it became more SHARP, very much more street-oriented. And then it became just another group of skinheads. . . . Part of that was because the Trotskyists and other factions were trying to use us, to get us just to be their, their muscle. . . . We didn't want anything to do with that. . . . And so, everybody was like: we're just going to fight them [nazis] in the street, and keep it there."[107] In Mic Crenshaw's assessment, this was a self-conscious return to the subculture's origins: "Rose City Bovver Boys and other formations were rooted in being a skinhead first."[108]

But for Pan, one of the Bovver Boys' founders, it was also partly a reinterpretation of that tradition, brought on by a change in scene: "I moved to L.A. and I got a whole different orientation down in L.A. of gang life."[109] He realized then, "Rude Boys are hard as hell, man; they're like straight-up gangsters."[110] That insight carried over into the new group: "When I came back, and we started Rose City [Bovver Boys], it was just straight gang life."[111] This was another way of connecting to the rude boy origins: "I mean, that was sort of what Rose City was about. . . . Like, we wanted to be hard as nails, but the best dressed."[112]

Break-Up and Renewal

By the turn of the century, ARA was in transition. Some members were aging out, with adult responsibilities, families, and full-time jobs.[113] Others were exhausted and traumatized. "We could not keep doing this," one former member explains. "You can only keep doing this for so long. People got arrested. People went to prison. People got stabbed. People got shot at. People got shot."[114]

At the same time, for a variety of reasons, the radical right was itself in a period of stagnation.[115] And for ARA, a group built on direct confrontation, victory posed its own difficulties. "[W]here there is not a visible or active nazi presence, ARA groups fell into a state of inactivity," Rory McGowan later wrote, noting too that, while predictable, that only revealed the group's final "inability to connect anti-racism with other struggles." It wasn't for lack of trying. In the first years of the new century, ARA still had several hundred members throughout the country, and they increasingly put their energy into the radical wing of the antiglobalization movement, organizing against the police, and defending mosques after September 11, 2001. ARA members took part in some of the most visible manifestations of popular discontent in the period, including the 1999 Seattle demonstrations against the World Trade Organization and the 2001 Cincinnati riots against police brutality.[116]

But during this same period, several ARA groups were breaking apart as a result of their own internal dynamics, especially a stubborn misogyny. Over the previous decade, increasing numbers of women, queers, and younger people had entered the movement and resented the sexist attitudes common among the original cohort. "There would be tension around some of the members of ARA calling Nazis pussies or faggots," Katrina, a former member from Minneapolis, explains.[117] Several chapters found themselves embroiled in messy processes attempting to deal with sexual assault.[118] "Some [women] left in plain disgust at the macho behavior of some ARA men," McGowan recalls. At the national conference in 1998, the network as a whole suffered a major split because of sexism. RASH, which was ARA-affiliated, split into East Coast and Midwest factions soon after, only then to split again.[119]

Antifa emerged during this period of reconfiguration and reorientation. The first of the new organizations, North East Antifascists—whose name was commonly, if informally, rendered "Northeastern Antifa"—was founded in Boston in 2002. Though commonly working with ARA, it was never formally affiliated and adopted the "Antifa" label partly to signal the influence of the European antifascist movement and partly because its members wanted to take a broader approach and give more attention to institutional racism and to racism on the left. A few years later, Rose City Antifa, in Portland, followed suit.[120]

In 2013, several former ARA groups affiliated to form the Torch Antifa Network. The Torch website insists that the shift came as

"NOT a fracture or schism coming from internal strife" but growing out of "changes in the current political climate," as well as in "our own political development, our understanding of what fascism is and how it relates to other political entities such as the working class, capital, and the state."[121] Torch intended to drop some of ARA's baggage and continue the work with a more feminist politics and an approach increasingly inspired by European antifascist groups.[122]

The results of this change in direction have been rather mixed and in at least two respects disappointing. Though a queer and feminist presence is ever more visible within antifascist circles, macho attitudes and casual misogyny undeniably persist and in some groups still predominate.[123] And, despite the desire of Northeastern Antifa's founders to take a broader approach than ARA, by 2021 Antifa-brand politics had become undeniably *narrower* than ARA's had been. ARA took up issues as varied as police violence, reproductive rights, prisoner support, and Palestinian solidarity. Antifa groups are much more specialized, focusing almost exclusively on countering the far right.[124]

Whatever the changes, though, there was a definite sense of continuity. Torch's points of unity were patterned on ARA's:

1. We disrupt fascist and far right organizing and activity.

2. We don't rely on the cops or courts to do our work for us. . . .

3. We oppose all forms of oppression and exploitation. . . .

4. We hold ourselves accountable personally and collectively to live up to our ideals and values.

5. We not only support each other within the network, but we also support people outside the network who we believe have similar aims or principles. An attack on one is an attack on all.[125]

By 2021, Torch had nine chapters in seven states.[126] But, more significantly, there were a far greater number of unaffiliated Antifa groups throughout the country. Torch is, in a sense, a relic of the ARA "network" model, while the overall movement has shifted more toward discreet, autonomous collectives. Many of these are completely informal, with no fixed structure or definite membership, and they coordinate (or not) as needed for specific projects or actions.[127]

Despite or because of its nebulous structure, *Antifa* has become a specter haunting the imaginations of the Fox News crowd, who use the word to refer without distinction to anyone with vaguely progressive political views and to black bloc protesters in particular.[128] As a consequence *Antifa* is now a household word, though its politics are generally misunderstood and its prominence greatly exaggerated. Far from being the Soros-financed paramilitary somehow devoted simultaneously to a Marxist ideology and to the Democratic National Committee, Antifa groups are typically small collectives, volunteer-run, poorly funded, ideologically eclectic, and as much opposed to the neoliberal state as to the fascist movement that seeks to replace it. That antifascists can generate so much attention yet continue to be so badly misjudged speaks volumes about the right's propaganda machine—and about the left's failure to match it. That sort of failure tends to spiral. The malignant and distorted image of Antifa in the popular imagination is both a cause and a consequence of its relative isolation. That isolation, in turn, represents a serious vulnerability and a major political shortcoming. It has become fuel for the far right, who habitually exaggerate Antifa's violence in order to justify their own.

Skinheads and Scapegoats (Reconsidered)

The skinhead has always been an ambiguous figure, his image assembled from the remnants of a decaying working class and the innovations of recent immigrants, mediating the contradictory impulses of mod fashion and proletarian practicality, expressing both alienation and a deep sense of community. Over time, the image only became more fraught. To the public at large, the skinhead was almost an embodiment of racial hatred and mindless violence. To a certain type of initiate, however, he stood as a heroic model of working-class pride and resistance to racial oppression.

But heroes and villains are as much the products of history as its creators. The murder of Mulugeta Seraw, as Elinor Langer demonstrates in *A Hundred Little Hitlers*, occurred less as a result of WAR's organizing than because Oregon's history and culture provided fertile ground for white supremacist beliefs to grow—from Indian wars, to Black exclusion laws, to pogroms against the Chinese, to the Klan's control of government, to Japanese internment, and a nearly unbroken legacy of housing discrimination and police brutality.

But after Seraw's murder, the public was in no mood for sociological treatises. They wanted a morality play, with ready-made villains whose punishment could assuage the community's collective guilt. The adolescent malcontents in East Side White Pride fit the bill perfectly. The figure of the skinhead provided a caricatured image of racism, safely removed from the operations of respectable society. "A thick wall of righteousness simultaneously depressing in its self-delusion and touching in its goodwill was now found to be separating 'Us'—the good people—from 'Them'—the bad skinheads," Langer wrote.[129]

The role of the *antiracist* skinhead in countering the nazis ironically reinforced this impression in the public imagination and allowed the authorities to depict the whole ugly conflict as a particularly virulent species of juvenile delinquency.[130] By this way of thinking, skinhead violence was a criminal rather than political phenomenon, a matter for the police with no significance for the larger society. That is a comforting illusion and only more dangerous for being so comforting.

Thirty years after the height of the skinhead wars, the right is resurgent. Those opposing it, all now labeled "Antifa" by reactionary agitators and bewildered journalists, are again being criminalized by police, denounced by liberals, and physically attacked by men who openly fantasize about death squads.[131] These days the fascist shock troops are older, less lumpen, and—in a word—*square*. But they are, for all of that, still very dangerous, and the resemblance to their forebears may prove to be more important than the differences.

Sometimes, in fact, there is no difference. It is the *same people*. Among the mob swarming the Oregon Capitol on January 6, 2021—simultaneous with the assault on the U.S. Capitol—was Kyle Brewster, one of the skinheads who murdered Mulugeta Seraw.[132]

Part Three: Proud Boys as Alt-Gang

Origins and Orientation

Of the numerous groups that have emerged from the recent wave of rightwing activity, the most visible at the national level has probably been the Proud Boys.

In 2016, *Vice* magazine founder Gavin McInnes set out to harness the alienated male rage expressing itself in the internet's trolling culture and convert it into a real-world organization with a street presence and a fighting capacity. So, as he succinctly put it in an interview with Joe Rogan, "I started this gang called the Proud Boys."[133]

He wrote in an essay announcing the group, "What began as a few fans [of McInnes's podcast] in a bar across the street from the studio singing 'Proud of Your Boy' and laughing at the reparations videos of Gazi Kodzo soon became a bona fide men's club with rituals, traditions, and even its own in-house court called 'The Sharia.'"[134] Within weeks the Proud Boys claimed a dozen chapters and an estimated thousand members.[135] "Though the exact details are kept secret," McInnes writes coyly, "the meetings usually consist of drinking, fighting, and reading aloud from Pat Buchanan's *Death of the West*."[136]

Almost at once, the Proud Boys—recognizable by their signature black-and-gold Fred Perry tennis shirts—became a fixture of the left-right street battles regularly occurring in American cities. In August 2017, some members joined the "Unite the Right" rally in Charlottesville. McInnes warned them ahead of time not to advertise their affiliation: "Just don't fucking wear your Fred Perry, or decide to belt: 'Proud of Your Boy.' . . . If you decide to rub elbows with those people [while] in colors, you very well could find yourself being disavowed."[137] This reluctance was strange since the rally's principal organizer, Jason Kessler, was a member of the Virginia chapter and had appeared on *The Gavin McInnis Show* a few weeks before to promote the event.[138] After the day turned deadly, McInnes sought to control the damage to his brand, publishing one of his signature essay-decrees titled "We Are Not Alt-Right." He immediately expelled Kessler and further declared, "all white nationalist/anti-Semites are banned from Proud Boys."[139]

"The two big differences" between the Proud Boys and the Alt-Right, McInnes wrote, are "the 'JQ' [Jewish Question] and racial identity politics": "They think the Jews are responsible for America's problems and they think 'Western' is inseparable from 'white.' They don't see a future for non-whites in America. FUCK THAT. We reject all of those things. We openly encourage Jewish and non-white members and want them to know they're at home with us."[140]

Despite McInnes's protestations, Proud Boys routinely traffic in the symbols of the Alt-Right milieu, including Pepe the Frog imagery and the "okay" hand sign.[141] And while it is true that the group welcomes men of many races and any sexuality, that sense of inclusiveness is somewhat undercut by the tendency of its members to shout racist and homophobic slurs at people, especially when literally kicking them on the ground.[142]

In mid-2016, McInnes described the group and its politics this way: "The Proud Boys are over race . . . we don't have any guilt. No guilt whatsoever. No cis male guilt, none of that stuff. We're pro-gun. We want to end the drug war . . . we're libertarians, except when it comes to immigration. We are pro-dude. We think most women would be happier at home. . . . We are traditionalists. We're sort of like the alt-right without the racism."[143]

In truth, the Proud Boys' racial politics are more ambiguous than McInnes lets on. By concentrating on "Western" rather than "white," McInnes has shifted the racist criteria from color to culture, which turns out to be a substantive reconceptualization, entailing different commitments and emphasizing different oppositions.[144] Rather than promote an identity based on militant whiteness—defined, in large part, by anti-Black racism—the Proud Boys imagine a unified West, cast in special opposition to Islam. Domestically, the main enemy is not Blacks or Jews but Antifa—where "Antifa" includes anyone who might oppose their program: liberals, socialists, feminists, even journalists who report on the movement critically.[145] This reconfiguration leaves the narrative structure of white supremacy intact but places it on a new foundation and thus alters its precise content but not its overall spirit.[146]

McInnes was once invited by a white nationalist interviewer to recite the famous "Fourteen Words" composed by The Order's David Lane—"We must secure the existence of our people and a future for white children"—which the Anti-Defamation League calls "the most popular white supremacist slogan in the world."[147] McInnes accommodated the request, with one adjustment. He replaced *white* with *Western*.[148] This sort of teasing flirtation with the far right was typical of his leadership. It produced a pattern of oscillation just at the edges of white nationalism, with a simultaneous dialogue between the leadership and the base: the rank-and-file members move ever closer to white supremacists, with a predictable escalation in violence, until some normative line is crossed and the public outraged; the leadership then denounces the action, distances the group from the swastika set, and disciplines individual members—all while denying their own responsibility.[149]

Rightwing Gang Culture

If nothing else, the Proud Boys' gender politics are crystal clear. Openly nostalgic for a patriarchy and aggressively anti-trans, they blame feminism and the left for sidelining men and weakening Western society. "Like Archie Bunker," McInnes writes, they "long for the days when 'girls were girls and men were men.'"[150]

Central to their efforts to valorize masculinity in general—and to assert their own masculinity, especially—there is an exaggerated inclination toward violence. "Fighting solves everything," McInnes likes to say.[151] Violence is, to a large degree, what their group is about. At the very least, it is foundational to their self-presentation. Some Proud Boys T-shirt designs shows a pair of brass knuckles with each loop containing one of the initials POYB (for "Proud of Your Boy") or a fist with POYB on the knuckles.[152]

"We will kill you," McInnes boasted on his podcast in mid-2016. "That's the Proud Boys in a nutshell. We will kill you."[153]

While their chosen nemesis is certainly Antifa, intra-group violence is also a part of the Proud Boys' culture. Their very first meeting, in a Brooklyn bar in 2016, erupted into a spontaneous fistfight between two members—a "young punk" and a "suit." "It's funny, there was a big fist fight," McInnes later told an interviewer. "One of them was covered in blood at the end. I guess in a way, it showed the range of the membership."[154] This is a rather remarkable response. It casts internal violence as a sign of the group's diversity, the assumption being that even minor differences will result in bloodshed and thus that the tolerance for violence is a sign of inclusivity. More likely, of course, is that the threat of violence comes to pervade the whole atmosphere of the organization, shaping every interaction and producing a culture of bullying.[155]

Violence is a source of status within the group. Of the organization's four degrees of membership, three involve a physical ordeal, and two require actual violence. The First Degree is achieved just by declaring oneself a Proud Boy and uttering a simple oath: "I'm a proud Western chauvinist, and I refuse to apologize for creating the modern world."[156] To earn the Second Degree, McInnes explains: "You must get the crap beaten out of you by at least five guys until you can name five breakfast cereals."[157] The Third Degree requires being tattooed or branded with a Proud Boys symbol.[158]

The Fourth Degree was added in early 2017.[159] It is reserved for members who have "endured a major conflict related to the cause." Early on, McInnes openly described this in terms of "kicking the crap out of antifa," though he later played that off as a "joke" and offered this (non-)clarification: "This obviously doesn't mean you go to someone's house or even pick a fight with one at a rally. If you do such a thing, that's 100% on you and has nothing to do with the group's tenets. It's about defending yourself. We don't start fights, we finish them. 4th degree is a consolation prize for being thrust into a shitty situation and surviving."[160]

Of course, picking fights at rallies is exactly the group's established modus operandi, and it has developed into a means of advancing to leadership. One Proud Boy, Ethan Nordean (who also uses the nickname Rufio Panman), achieved internet fame after he was filmed disarming an antifascist activist and near-simultaneously knocking him unconscious with a single punch.[161] Nordean was later made sergeant-at-arms for the Seattle chapter.[162] He is now one of the select group of "elders" responsible for guiding the organization at a national level.[163]

But McInnes was walking a tricky line. He cherished the group's aggressive, transgressive reputation but also the image that they were just a bunch of regular guys, drinking beer and roughhousing. Likewise, he wanted to present his boys as battle-hardened and bad-ass but *also* to depict their violence (against all evidence) as purely defensive, though absolutely decisive. To do this, he needed to deploy two types of stories simultaneously: a victim narrative and a victory narrative.[164] In both stories, violence is central to the group's self-image and to the image that it wishes to project. As criminologist Shannon E. Reid explains, this propensity for violence—and as important, their violent *reputation*—attracts recruits and supplies a kind of "mythology" that helps to cement group cohesion: "[It] helps build their identity and is sort of central to the in-group/out-group dynamic and group ethos that binds people together."[165]

McInnes may (or may not) have been kidding when he described the Proud Boys as a gang.[166] His shtick is exactly this continuous flow of half-serious, exaggerated, and contradictory statements, along with in-jokes and blatant absurdities, all thrown together under the banner of irony.[167]

However he intended the comment, numerous observers have considered the gang label exactly the right one.[168] The criminologists Shannon Reid and Matthew Valasik, for example, call the Proud Boys "a prototypical Alt-Right gang," citing numerous features that the group shares with "conventional street gangs." Among these are "a collective identity," regular in-group socializing, clothing with identifying colors, "hand signals (i.e., the 'OK' sign)," a "violent initiation ritual," distinctive tattoos, individual and collective recourse to violence, "a loose organizational structure," and a "female auxiliary" (Proud Boys' Girls). The scholars also note the motivating force of a violent inter-gang rivalry: "Much of the Proud Boys' hateful rhetoric and violence is aimed at Antifa . . . a pattern no different than the violent rivalries between racist skinheads groups and traditional street gangs." Furthermore: "As with conventional street gangs, Proud Boys appeal to marginalized men who feel they have no place in modern society." Reid and Valasik suggest that the main thing preventing police, researchers, and the public from understanding the Proud Boys as a gang is a racist stereotype about what gangs are like and who is in them.[169] Reid told an interviewer: "Law enforcement is conditioned to see their enemy as Black and Brown people, and that 'gangs' are groups of Black and Brown people."[170]

Given their far-right politics, cult of masculine violence, and gang personae, it may not be surprising to discover that some of the specifics of Proud Boy culture signal a conscious borrowing from the skinheads. Fred Perry shirts have long also been the favorite of both racist and antiracist skinheads.[171] Skinhead imagery—including tattoos, stickers, patches, and the like—often features the Fred Perry laurel wreaths, which also appear in the Proud Boys logo.[172] Some Proud Boy T-shirts feature pictures of Doc Martens, the classic skinhead boots. McInnes himself sports a tattoo, and sometimes clothing, referencing that most infamous and influential nazi skinhead band, Skrewdriver.[173]

Sometimes the crossover is more than just a cultural appropriation. The *Guardian* reports: "At least three of those who participated [with the Proud Boys] in a gang assault in New York in 2018 were affiliated with racist skinhead crews long known to local antifascist and antiracist organizers, like the 211 Bootboys, a far-right skinhead gang based mostly in New York City, and Battalion 49 (B49), a predominantly Latino neo-Nazi skinhead gang."[174] The incident in question is interesting and important, not only for what it shows of the Proud Boys' politics but also because it led to McInnes's formal departure from the group he founded.

On the night of October 12, 2018, as they left the Metropolitan Republican Club on the Upper East Side of Manhattan, having viewed a presentation in which Gavin McInnes reenacted the assassination of a Japanese socialist and urged the audience to "never let evil take root," a group of Proud Boys encountered a smaller group of antifascists and literally stomped them.[175] Ten of McInnes's minions were arrested. Two were later convicted of attempted gang assault, attempted assault, and riot; they were sentenced to four years. Seven others pled to lesser charges.[176]

A few weeks later, on November 21, McInnes announced that he was leaving the organization, a move he described as "100% a legal gesture" intended to "show jurors they are not dealing with a gang and there is no head of operations."[177]

McInnes was briefly replaced by Jason Lee Van Dyke, a former prosecutor who sometimes served as the Proud Boys' attorney. He resigned two days later, after accidently publishing a list of the group's governing "elders." (Since leaving the group, Van Dyke has been arrested for filing a false police report, and his license to practice law was suspended after he threatened violence against a man he was suing. He tried to join the neo-Nazi terrorist organization The Base but was rejected as representing a "huge liability.")[178] Van Dyke was replaced by Henry "Enrique" Tarrio, an Afro-Cuban Proud Boy who once headed the Miami chapter.[179]

Then, in 2021, the organization entered into another period of crisis. At least thirty people connected with the Proud Boys—including prominent leaders like Ethan Nordean and Joe Biggs—were arrested for their role in the January 6 Capitol Hill putsch.[180] Tarrio, the sitting chairman, was arrested in DC shortly *before* the attack, after trying to illegally sell two high-capacity magazines marked with the Proud Boys logo.[181]

After his arrest, Reuters revealed that Tarrio had worked for almost ten years as an informant for both the Miami police and the FBI, leading to more than a dozen prosecutions related to drugs, gambling, and human smuggling. Tarrio initially denied cooperating with the authorities but also said that he routinely informed police of the Proud Boys' plans in advance of their rallies.[182] These revelations fed suspicion within the organization, leading some to denounce Tarrio as "a rat" and call for his removal.[183]

(Proud) Boys in Blue

This sudden distrust of law enforcement was ironic, as the Proud Boys had long enjoyed what the SPLC described as a "cozy relationship with the police."[184] Anecdotal evidence from around the country would seem to justify the claim.

In Vancouver, Washington, in 2018, when Proud Boys riding in a pickup truck adorned with a Confederate flag jumped a Black teenager, cops arrested the teenager.[185] Soon after, in the surrounding jurisdiction of Clark County, a sheriff's deputy was fired after she appeared online modeling Proud Boys' Girls merchandise.[186] The following year, an officer in East Hampton, Connecticut, abruptly retired after it was revealed that he was a member of the Proud Boys, though the police chief said membership in the group did not violate department policy.[187] Around the same time, a Plaquemines Parish sheriff's deputy was fired after posting on social media about his Proud Boys membership; he was one of the people responsible for vetting new members for the Louisiana chapter.[188] In Oregon, also in 2019, a contractor with Immigration and Customs Enforcement posted bail for a Proud Boy who had been arrested for assault.[189]

In the spring of 2020, the Chicago police opened an investigation into one of their officers after it was discovered that he posted to an online Proud Boy message board titled "Fuck Antifa." There he helped organize meetings, bragged about using his law enforcement connections to track antifascists, and claimed he was working behind the scenes to get Antifa declared a terrorist organization.[190] That summer, about ten Proud Boys were photographed—in their colors—at a party at the Fraternal Order of Police headquarters in Philadelphia.[191] Soon thereafter, while responding to racial justice protests in Los Angeles, a National Guard sergeant posted a photo of himself, in battle dress, displaying his weapon, standing in front of a military vehicle that had been marked with the Proud Boy tag "POYB."[192]

Meanwhile, in Portland, "the epicenter" for left/right clashes during the Trump years,[193] police routinely traded information with rightwing organizers and shielded their fighters from arrest—most notably Tusitala "Tiny" Toese, a notorious Proud Boy brawler.[194] In contrast, the same cops have repeatedly attacked antifascist counterprotesters without provocation.[195] Asked about the difference, a police lieutenant explained that the rightwing demonstrators were "much more mainstream."[196] Criminologists Reid and Valasik have accused the Portland Police of responding to the Proud Boys with "apathy."[197] Others—including city council member Jo Ann Hardesty—have used the word "collusion."[198]

After Proud Boys leader Joe Biggs was arrested for his role in the Capitol siege, it was revealed that he had been recruited by the FBI to provide information on Antifa and that he had regularly informed the FBI and the Portland police about demonstrations he was helping organize there. "These talks were intended to inform law enforcement about Proud Boy activities in Portland on a courtesy basis," Biggs's attorney told the court, "but also to ask for advice on planned marches or demonstrations." In exchange, Biggs received "cautionary" messages from federal agents, presumably about Antifa's plans.[199]

Back in New York, McInnes himself liked to brag, "I have a lot of support in the NYPD and I very much appreciate that, the boys in blue."[200] One inside account portrayed the police as essentially providing security for the Proud Boys' "Pro-Trump Bar Crawl" in 2018. Uniformed officers guarded the doors; one recommended that the organizer stop tweeting the group's location, fearing interference from Antifa; and a plainclothes officer checked in to make sure the group was having fun, offering amiably, "Let us know if you need anything."[201]

The warm feeling was mutual. In fact, it appears that the Proud Boys sometimes saw themselves not merely as supporters of the police or as allies but as adjuncts. In 2017, Proud Boys member Kyle Chapman—nicknamed "Based Stickman" after appearing in a video striking an antifascist protester with a club—announced that he was forming a "tactical defense arm" called the Fraternal Order of the Alt-Knights (FOAK). An article on the Proud Boys website explained: "The need for defense has grown since recent premeditated attacks by the radical Marxist group 'Anti-Fa' have become the norm at any cultural event politically to the right of Jane Fonda. . . . FOAK will now take the next logical step in organizing the Proud Boy watchdogs into a force to protect and serve when the police are told to stand down."[202]

Despite these affinities, the occasional collusion, and overlapping membership, by 2021 the cops–Proud Boys honeymoon seemed to be over. Rightwing attacks on the government—state capitols and then, most spectacularly, the U.S. Capitol—led to violent clashes with police and then to systematic arrests. For many among the Proud Boys, the fact that the police would suddenly hold a line against them was met with feelings of dismay and betrayal. After being arrested for his role in the Capitol assault, Nordean complained, "[Even though] we've had their back for years, the police are starting to become a problem."[203]

Thug Reich

Questions about Tarrio's leadership drew internal divisions to the surface. At least five chapters left the national organization: Indiana first, followed by Alabama, Oklahoma, Missouri, and Nevada. "If other states follow this lead we can have a truly autonomous chapter that won't be liable for the mistakes of the next chairman or the next group of elders," Brien James urged on Telegram. "Don't talk about autonomy. Be autonomous."[204]

Unfortunately, a splintering may lead to even more extreme politics and more violent action.[205] James, in addition to being the state head of the Indiana Proud Boys and a former member of FOAK, also has a long history in the racist skinhead scene. He helped to start several racist gangs—Knightstown Boys, Outlaw Hammerskins, and Hoosier State Skinheads.[206] More recently, he helped to found the Vinlanders Social Club, bringing together the Hoosier State Skinheads, Ohio State Skinheads, and the Keystone State Skinheads with the aim of creating a "Thug Reich."[207]

It was not the first attempt to pull the Proud Boys in a more openly fascist direction. After McInnes resigned in 2016, Augustus Sol Invictus, the former second-in-command of the Alt-Knights, declared himself head of the larger organization and promised to rescind the prohibition on white supremacists and antisemites.[208]

Similarly, in November 2020, when Tarrio was filmed retreating after being slashed with a knife in a street fight, FOAK's Kyle Chapman challenged his leadership and declared himself "president of the Proud Boys effective immediately." He wrote: "We will no longer cuck to the left by appoint[ing] token negros as our leaders. We will no longer allow homosexuals or other 'undesirables' into our ranks. We recognize that the West was built by the White Race alone and we owe nothing to any other race."[209]

None of these efforts amounted to much, but they pointed to underlying—and unresolved—tensions.

Stand Back and Stand By

Meanwhile, as the Republican Party suffered its own crisis—divided not merely between a center right and a far right but also between an establishment and an insurgent orientation—the far-right insurgents, the wing of the party more loyal to Trump personally than to the constitutional system, increasingly allied with the Proud Boys and used them as muscle against other members of their own party.

Loyalty to Trump was always part of the Proud Boys' platform, but it received an ironic sort of blessing from the man himself in September 2020. In the course of the first presidential debate, when Trump was challenged to disavow the support of white supremacists, he asked for the name of a group. His opponent, Joe Biden, suggested the Proud Boys. Trump then immediately enjoined, "Proud Boys—stand back and stand by." This was, to say the least, not the firm denunciation that anyone may have been hoping for, and was instead widely interpreted as encouragement—not least by the Proud Boys themselves, who immediately produced a new logo incorporating the president's phrase as a slogan.[210] Two months later, when Biden's victory was announced, Enrique Tarrio posted to the group, "We're rolling out. . . . Standby order has been rescinded."[211]

Throughout Trump's term, the Proud Boys sometimes served as security at Republican Party events. The same month as the debate, September 2020, in Delaware, they worked a campaign event for Lauren Witzke, a Republican candidate for U.S. Senate who later publicly thanked them for protecting her from Black

Lives Matter and Antifa.[212] In October, they provided security for a public appearance by Congressman Matt Gaetz in Florida.[213] Most prominently, as early as 2018, Roger Stone—the sometime advisor and eager henchman to President Trump—hired the Proud Boys to serve as his security and even recited their initiation oath (though he denies being a member).[214]

As Trump was forced from office and the party divided into competing factions, the Proud Boys took on an internal policing role. Early in 2021, Tiny Toese, recently released from jail after being convicted of assault, began serving as the Clark County (Washington) Republican Party's unofficial sergeant-at-arms. At a February 23 meeting concerned mainly with a motion to censure congressional Republicans who had voted for impeachment, Toese was instructed to remove one member who voiced opposition to the proposal.[215]

In May 2021, Republicans in the Nevada state senate called for an investigation into their own party after reports that a bloc of forty Proud Boys were added to the membership roster in order to swing the vote on a resolution censuring the Secretary of State for "failing to investigate election fraud."[216] (One Proud Boy leader later bragged online, "Our votes absolutely made the difference.")[217] At the same time, the Clark County (Nevada) Republican Party expelled seven members for their associations with the Proud Boys, their racist and antisemitic internet posts, and their online harassment of female politicians. (Two elected officials, a judge and a school board trustee, both Republican women, reported threats.) The excluded members filed a discrimination suit against both the state and the county parties, and the Clark County Republicans cancelled their regular meeting, fearing disruption.[218]

Around the same time, on May 6, 2021, the Republican Party of Multnomah County, Oregon, held a secret meeting to recall its chairman, Stephen Lloyd, after he made statements to the effect that "diversity is an extremely important part of society" and that the party should be "open to everyone." The petition initiating the procedure called for a closed meeting at an undisclosed location, citing "the danger of Antifa."[219]

When the event took place, in a Northeast Portland church, security was organized by a well-known Proud Boy, Daniel Tooze, and his firm, Proud Security, Inc.[220] A neighbor later complained, "These 'patrols' were pure intimidation—they were drinking, shouting to each other, shining flashlights into our neighbors' homes and faces, and displaying weapons. They circled, harassed and threatened another neighbor on this street who was working out. They vandalized our block with Proud Boys stickers. . . . I was spit at, yelled at, and cursed at."[221]

At the following meeting, on May 17, Proud Boys were again providing security and refused to admit party members from the opposing caucus. As a result, each faction held separate meetings and elected competing chairmen, leaving the party in a state of internal confusion.[222]

Blackshirt Sentimentality

The Proud Boys are a peculiarly contradictory set. They are both transgressive and conventional, conservative and rebellious, libertarian and intolerant. Perhaps most perplexing, they are a multiracial white supremacist organization and an anti-immigrant group founded by an immigrant.[223] By shifting the focus from "white" to "The West" and emphasizing culture over biology, the Proud Boys have adopted a seemingly post-racial racism. But, as it turns out, there is functionally not much difference between a Western chauvinist fraternity and a white supremacist gang.[224]

One distinguishing feature of fascism is its faith in the redeeming power of violence—specifically its potential to restore a mythic order characterized by organic ties of community under the authority of an eternal hierarchy, providing each individual with a sense of identity, place, and purpose.[225] In terms of their public policy agenda, the Proud Boys mostly just repeat stock Republican talking points about ending immigration and preserving gun rights (as well as stopping Antifa).[226] But, at a deeper level, there is something of the fascist spirit animating the group. That spirit, which is precisely what makes them so dangerous, goes a long way toward explaining their special attraction. Disoriented and dislocated by shifts in national identity and gender relations—and perhaps especially unnerved by the challenges migration, multiculturalism, feminism, and queer politics pose to the very ideas of nationality and gender—the Proud Boys seek to reassert traditional hierarchies and reaffirm their sense of identity. As Alexandra Minna Stern explains in *Proud Boys and the White Ethnostate*: "Some alt-right fantasies . . . disclose a sentimental thirst for connection and community."[227]

This longing, which can find its expression in the idealized nationalism of fascist movements, may also find some psychological approximation in gang life. The gang offers both a place where you belong and a feeling that some place belongs to you. It provides a sense of camaraderie and self-worth *and* a vehicle for enacting violence in the service of a shared ideal or identity. In fact, these two aspects feed one another. Violence can help build group cohesion, but when a group defines itself through conflict with others, the very sense of identity can itself become the source for violence. That can be true for an individual, a crew, or a nation.

Part Four: Considerations

Influence and Inheritable Traits

In *Freedom Is an Endless Meeting*, her study of decision-making in leftwing social movements, the sociologist Francesca Polletta notes that new organizations often, consciously or not, pattern themselves on relationships with which the participants already have some comfortable familiarity—such as friend groups, religious congregations, and college seminars. These models provide norms that help set expectations, structure interactions, and mitigate potential conflicts. Especially early on, the chosen template may be the thing that provides enough common understanding for the group to function at all, without having to improvise and negotiate at every moment.[228] However, once that governing pattern is set, it can be extremely difficult to adjust, and groups tend to enter crises when their political ambitions run up against the limits of their implicit structure.[229]

Polletta is particularly concerned with the practices of direct democracy in activist organizations, but I think the implications of her theory are much more expansive and likely affect every part of an organization in one way or another. Sometimes the effects of the given model will be direct and linear, but often they will be more subtle, forming a set of unconscious dispositions that together make it more likely that ideas or practices will be adopted if they fit with the original pattern.

For more than thirty years, the American antifascist movement has sought to maintain a militant edge while moving away from the gang model—first in the jump from the Baldies to ARA, then in the shift from ARA to Antifa. Nevertheless, though it is in no way the only or even the main source or influence shaping antifascist organizing today, the gang element has left a deep imprint. It shows up in some relatively benign cultural signifiers, like laurel-wreath imagery, the use of tattoos as markers of loyalty, and a greater-than-average enthusiasm for soccer and ska.[230] It also shows up in some minor tactical choices, such as the use of graffiti to "mark space as antifascist or reclaim it from fascists."[231]

It is important here to acknowledge the inherent attractions of the gang as a social unit, the very real needs it can fill in the lives of its members, and the advantages these can bring for political action. Looking back over his long experience with antiracist organizing, Mic Crenshaw concludes: "I think what made us strong . . . is that we were friends and we loved each other, and we approached the struggle and the activity from that basis. . . . When you take away the overt political ideologies and the violence, it was really about friendship. When I founded the Baldies, that was the first time I really felt at home."[232]

Yet even this sense of belonging and the mutual loyalty that it engenders can involve some important trade-offs. The sense of cohesion and group identity can foster insularity, which can sometimes lead to groupthink and even a kind of cultishness. Combine that with the security requirements related to organized violence, and together these factors can promote a suspicion of outsiders that limits growth, hinders the ability to form alliances, and may keep the movement both isolated and fragmented.[233]

A Confrontational Style

The most important inheritance from the gang culture is the attitude toward violence. "Antifa culture venerates confrontation," Stanislav Vysotsky explains, "often relying on aggressive and violent imagery." This militancy, Vysotsky argues repeatedly, is what makes Antifa what it is, even when no actual violence ensues. "When antifa activists engage in non-militant tactics, they do so in a manner that is often aggressive and confrontational. . . . The militant antifascist style of activism takes on a confrontational tone even when applied to non-militant tactics."[234] It is precisely "the style with which they deploy these tactics" that "distinguishes militant antifascists from their non-militant comrades" and "differentiates them from other more mainstream antifascists." Crucially for our purposes, Vysotsky suggests that as much as antifascist activists may be motivated by an "anti-authoritarian ideology," their confrontational "style" is largely "a product of their . . . subculture background."[235]

The gang's emphasis on physical courage and its readiness for combat clearly helped to inform ARA's (and, later, Antifa's) confrontational politics. But the "go where they go" ethos can unfortunately tend toward a fetishizing of direct confrontation, or even violence, to the exclusion of any consideration of other tactics. If the willingness to fight really is the thing that sets Antifa-type groups apart from antiracist organizing, it makes sense that people in those groups might develop an exaggerated sense of its importance: "Tactics," Vysotsky reminds us, "take on a life of their own as they become core signifiers of identity and belief."[236] The problem, then, is that tactics come to be selected not so much for strategic reasons but almost as a matter of aesthetics—for what they symbolize rather than what they achieve. "Saying that one is willing to directly engage with white nationalists is, by and large, a statement about their commitment to challenging the threat posed by fascism," Shane Burley observes, "but it doesn't answer whether direct confrontation is always the correct strategic choice."[237]

Risks and Ambiguities

Fascists must be opposed, sometimes with real violence. The martial virtues obviously have their place, but they always carry the risk of distorting the movement's culture and overall politics.[238] "Any movement that engages with violence must remain vigilant against the tendency for the violence to overtake political goals," Mark Bray cautions.[239] According to one ARA organizer, some chapters fell into this trap early in the twenty-first century. A "culture of insurrectionary machismo became more central," and the organization "started to feel like a highly political gang" that was "more into fighting than winning."[240]

Sometimes militancy becomes too identified with radicalism: it is assumed that violent tactics are always the most radical. Once that happens, it is a short step to *substituting* militancy for radicalism, which then tends toward an embrace of violence as an end rather than a means. Peter Little, a veteran of the movement, laments, "There's a difference between strategic militance and militance for its own sake. Without some political development . . . it's very easy to direct that energy in ways that become self-defeating, self-destructive, or just aren't effective."[241]

Moreover, an unfocused militancy can create its own problems. As violence becomes familiar, and as it brings rewards in terms of status or self-esteem, some people will gain a taste for it and engage in it in an undisciplined fashion, even for recreational purposes.[242] (It is worth taking seriously the first half of the common Antifa tag-line, "Sometimes anti-social, always antifascist.")[243] Moral questions aside, such bad habits bring the movement unnecessary casualties, arrests, and reputational costs, and they may pollute its internal dynamics with the threat of internecine violence. Individuals and groups may be tempted to use force to settle disputes within the movement (sometimes in a single organization), when matters might be better resolved through debate, negotiation, or even a tolerant indifference.[244] Once violence is accepted as a means, it may be difficult to limit the ends to which it will be put.

Alongside its inherent problems, a macho culture can also leave a group vulnerable to manipulation, either through direct infiltration or COINTELPRO-style disinformation campaigns designed to escalate inter- or intra-group rivalries to the point of violent conflict.[245]

A related problem is the mistaking of military questions for political questions, and thus military leadership for political leadership, tending toward exactly the sort of strongman politics the antifascist movement is intended to oppose. One might even discern an uncomfortable parallel between the left and the right in this respect: the emphasis on confrontation fosters the lionization of those who engage in violence, and violence then becomes a means for gaining status.[246] Unchecked, these tendencies can shape the overall culture, and thus the politics, of an organization or a movement. In *Confronting Fascism*, Don Hamerquist worried, "Some punks and skinheads who view themselves as working class revolutionaries, some elements of RASH, and even some participants in our own anti-fascist organizations are ambiguous on issues which should clearly differentiate right from left. These ambiguities, and actually this may be too mild a term, include romanticized views of violence, male supremacy, susceptibility to cults of omniscient leadership, and macho opposition to open debate and discussion with respect for individual and group autonomy."[247]

The kind of martial culture that I'm describing tends to foster a tough-guy aesthetic and a chauvinist politics. Dag, a Norwegian antifascist, writes, "Wherever violence is part of the political struggle you will have problems with machismo."[248] Mark Bray confirms: "No matter the country, my interviewees were unanimous about the problem of machismo, especially in the eighties and nineties."[249] Mic Crenshaw traces this attitude back to the movement's subcultural origins: "The skinhead culture is male-dominated, everything centered around the tough guy."[250] Naturally, there have been numerous attempts to address the scene's sexism, some reaching back decades, but they have yet to achieve anything like full success.[251]

The movement is left struggling to balance its political vision and its cultural traditions while simultaneously needing to retain its capacity for violence without fetishizing it. Some of these problems will arise in any movement that develops a fighting capacity.[252] Others are inherent to covert activities of any sort, even nonviolent ones. And it would be too much to suggest that every Antifa group exhibits these faults, though I do think the risks are always present. It would likewise be too simple to suggest that the gang background *created* these problems in any straightforward manner. But it certainly seems likely and, from a modest distance, even intuitive that the gang legacy has done much to shape the specific ways these dynamics manifest and the ways that they are resolved—or not.[253]

An Asymmetrical Conflict

On these matters, the Proud Boys face far fewer dilemmas. In principle, their thuggish organization is perfectly suited to their thuggish mind-set, their thuggish activities, and their thuggish political vision. They have achieved a perfect identity of form and content. Male violence is a theme uniting every level.

The gang form—the structure, the culture, the public presentation, the psychology of the members—is more congruent with the politics of the far right than it ever can be with the politics of the far left. It is of course not the only form that rightwing politics can take, and, as we have seen, some gangs have had leftwing commitments. But to the degree that an organization is gang-like, the mode of organization tends to distort leftwing politics, while it grounds fascist politics in the practices of daily life.

Yet, as the Proud Boys have discovered, a culture of bluster and fisticuffs is also limiting, especially in terms of discipline and strategy. Their leaders are continuously negotiating between the belligerent theatrics of their members and the limits to what society will tolerate. Repeatedly, up-front violence like that of Unite the Right, the Metropolitan Republican brawl, and the Capitol Hill putsch has precipitated crises in the organization and sometimes abrupt changes of leadership. Unfortunately, these inherent limitations do not make such gangs any less dangerous, and when their political frustrations become especially acute, it may push them toward even greater violence.

The Question of Violence and the Question of the State

While the antifascist movement's common sense embraces a "diversity of tactics," leaving space for both militant and nonviolent action, the real implications of violence penetrate far beneath the tactical level, touching on matters of strategy, organization, culture, and ultimately the movement's political direction.

The recourse to violence, Vysotsky argues, contains an implicit radicalism: "Antifascist militancy ultimately challenges the monopoly on the legitimate use of force reserved for the state and enacted by law enforcement. As a result, antifa activism represents a direct challenge to the very essence of the state."[254] Antifa is, under Vysotsky's description, "a form of radical community protection and social control," which means that "the defensive activities engaged in by antifa activists replicate some of the duties of law enforcement." By this interpretation, the very thing that constitutes a radical challenge to the state also leads Antifa to adopt practices like those of the state and contains an ever-present potential to develop in directions absolutely counter to the movement's liberatory aims. This contradiction is neatly captured in the title of the sixth chapter of his book: "Anarchy Police."[255]

Vysotsky tries to give this paradox the best possible spin, suggesting that "the proactive activity of militant antifascism presents an anti-authoritarian model for engaging in community protection" and that it is "consistent with general anarchist principles of spontaneity, direct democracy, direct action, and prefigurative practice."[256] It therefore "not only challenges the state's claim to a legitimate monopoly on the use of force, but also prefigures a framework for community safety and self-defense that is an alternative to existing police structures."[257] Specifically, he argues, "By acting spontaneously, the antifascist action is performed in a manner that prevents any individual or group from holding unwarranted power in this situation because participation in the confrontation is open to anyone. Although the use of force may be an exertion of power, it is one that is temporary and situational. The individuals engaging in militant antifascist confrontation and use of force are given no special status or social power, and their activity is certainly not institutionalized in any form, which gives them no overarching authority."[258]

This justification is weak on a number of points. While Vysotsky emphasizes the "directly democratic" nature of Antifa decision-making, he forgets that this form of democracy is entirely internal to the group using force and exerting power.[259] He neglects the problem of accountability to the broader movement— to say nothing of the communities in which antifascists operate. There may be no clear democratic mechanism for the movement as a whole to control its militant wing or even to quietly raise concerns.[260] Likewise, it is only dubiously reassuring to be told that violence is "spontaneous" and "open to anyone." (It is equally "open to anyone" to spontaneously take a rifle to a protest and declare oneself "security," but this increasingly common practice tends to create more problems than it solves.)[261] And the notion that the ability to successfully enact violence brings with it "no special sta-tus or social power" strains credulity. Anyone who has encountered a school bully knows otherwise. In sum, the notion that the "alter-native" to unaccountable institutionalized power is unaccountable deinstitutionalized power feels like an adjustment in the wrong direction.[262] The solution to the state's monopoly on violence is probably not to be found in unregulated entrepreneurial violence.

The difficulties here are numerous. The movement must main-tain a readiness for confrontation, even combat, without relying on it as a default. Violence must only be a means, used selectively. It must be constrained not only by our principles but also by some mechanism for democratic accountability.[263] Ideally, we would find a way of legitimating violence without normalizing it, reserving it for exceptional circumstances when the need is as real as the cost.[264] To build a movement that is capable of using violence strategically also means building a movement capable of directing and, when necessary, restraining its militant wing. It is not enough simply to defeat the enemy in combat; we also need to ensure that both the victory and the means used to achieve it are generally recognized as legitimate.

M. Treloar once warned against "thinking that the best way to fight fascism is to fight fascists."[265] Fighting fascists may be neces-sary, but it should never be the central aim. For one thing, the street fights are not likely to prove decisive. "I think that fundamentally this battle is going to be fought in people's workplaces, in their schools, in their churches," one former ARA member predicts.[266] Better then to develop a culture that makes fascism unacceptable and even unappealing, alongside a revolutionary program that cor-responds to people's real needs and draws any potential base away from the far right. As much as the conflict between fascism and antifascism might play out on the streets, success or failure will ultimately be determined in the political sphere.

Postscript

Neither Gangs nor Governments

Gang Radicalization

I started thinking about gangs because I was thinking about the police. The fact that the police use the strategy and techniques of counterinsurgency warfare in their fight against gangs led me, logically, to consider gangs as potential insurgents and to take gangs seriously as implicit and sometimes self-aware political actors. As thinking turned into writing and writing produced not one essay but three, I explored the subject in both historical and a contemporary contexts. In this admittedly incomplete examination, I have tried to give due weight to the benefits of gang formations—to the participants, to the communities in which they operate, and to social movements—as well as the risks and liabilities. I have paid particular attention to the *political* costs of gang activity, as opposed to the personal costs associated with violence, imprisonment, and the like.[1]

My conclusions, put bluntly, are these: The police use counterinsurgency to fight gangs not because gangs are inherently revolutionary but because they represent nascent (rival) states. Any effort to mobilize a gang for revolutionary change will face a number of problems, including the disruption of the organization's established business model, a lingering opportunistic and sometimes even predatory mind-set, resistance from within the gang, and the potential for increased repression. The greatest obstacles are those related to the gang's own culture. To become a force for liberation the organization will need to transcend the gang form. This transformation is difficult at best and will remain a struggle for several related reasons: the gang origin leaves an imprint on the culture of the organization; such groups have a tendency to revert to type; and failed insurgencies often decompose into simple criminality. Ultimately, I believe that the gang form fits more naturally with an authoritarian and rightwing politics than with a liberatory, leftwing politics. It will still face some inherent limitations, but in general there are fewer aspects of gang culture and gang activity that need to change when mobilizing in a reactionary direction.[2]

None of that should suggest that gang radicalization is either hopeless or counterproductive, but any such endeavor should be approached cautiously and without illusions.

Gangs, States, and the Left

That revolutionaries should be careful not to reproduce the logic of the state has been an accepted bit of anarchist doctrine since Bakunin's quarrel with Marx in the First International.[3] That we must also avoid patterning our organizations on gangs seems to have been less widely understood.

In the sixties, Black Mask (Up Against the Wall Motherfucker) defined the affinity group as "a street gang with analysis."[4] More recently, Bash Back liked to imagine themselves as gender-negating Droogs, the "ultraviolent" teenage hooligans from *A Clockwork Orange.*[5] *The Coming Insurrection*—once treated as a sacred text among a certain variety of anarchist—argues that the gang is an incipient type of commune, distinguished "only [by] a difference in scale."[6] And, most consequently, there is our inheritance from skinhead culture—the perennial temptation to fight fascist gangs with antifascist gangs.

We should take seriously Charles Tilly's observation that gangs and states belong on the same continuum. Whatever their ultimate purpose or aims, this continuity and the resemblances it suggests are, I think, better understood by both gangsters and cops than either would like to admit. It has a special significance, however, for insurgent social movements. Insurgents may be forced to operate outside the law yet must resist the tendency to drift toward venal criminal enterprises. Similarly, they may have to use coercion and violence to achieve their aims yet must avoid reproducing the dynamics of the state. Insurgent groups may not be able to renounce violence without also surrendering their political objectives; but equally, to preserve their liberatory politics, they cannot allow violence to become their central feature. The challenge for the revolutionary left—for any liberatory movement—is to break with the form of the criminal state, to establish our politics on an entirely new basis.

Too often on the left, debates about violence are simply debates about tactics, considered either from a moral or a pragmatic perspective. Pacifists renounce violence on principle; liberals denounce it hypocritically; and militants justify it on practical terms. The popularity of these various positions has tended to ebb and flow, but the debate itself is in stalemate. None of the arguments produced by any side seem likely to affect the position of the others, in part because they address themselves to different questions. The pacifist is mainly concerned with morality, the liberal with legality, and the militant with efficacy. With this debate always in the foreground, what receives less consideration is the question of *how* we organize violence: What types of groups engage in it? What norms govern it?

An Alternate Model

We can find the beginnings of an anarchist model in scott crow's "Liberatory Community Armed Self-Defense: Approaches towards a Theory." Inspired by examples like those of the Black Panthers and the Zapatistas, and critically reflecting on his own experiences with armed organizing in the aftermath of Hurricane Katrina and before that, with Anti-Racist Action, crow offers a definition of community defense as "the collective group practice of temporarily taking up arms for defensive purposes, as part of larger engagements of self-determination in keeping with liberatory ethics."[7] He tries to distinguish this sort of organization from several related but importantly different politico-military configurations, including militaries and police, guerrilla armies, paramilitaries and militias, terrorist groups, armed propaganda, and armed insurrections.[8] He puts forth this governing principle: "The armed component should never become the center. . . . To avoid that, and to equalize power as best we are able to, a liberatory analysis is necessary to nurture those who are learning to exercise their power, and for those who need to be accountable to their groups or communities."[9]

The characteristics crow identifies as setting community defense apart are fundamental, touching on questions of ideology, strategy, and organization. Ideologically, he says, "the liberatory framework is built on anarchist principles" such as mutual aid, direct action, solidarity, and "collective autonomy (community--self-determination)." Strategically, the objective is not "to seize state power" but to defend the social space in which communities may develop relationships and exercise power outside of the state's control. Organizationally, crow recommends "maintain[ing] a balance of power, [by] rotat[ing] all armed tasks and training among all those willing to participate." Likewise, the armed work needs to be integrated within the larger political project: "All firearms training needs to include dynamic and evolving liberatory ethics and practices in addition to how-to and safety." It follows too that violence ought never to be given primacy, either to the internal politics of the movement or in its relations with the broader society: "Those engaged with guns should hold the same power as others involved in other forms of community defense or self-sufficiency. Carrying arms should be seen as . . . [having] the same importance as child-care, growing food, or taking out the garbage—and not more." Even in narrowly defensive terms, the military capacity should not be the defining approach to political problems: "Arms are not the first line of defense and are only taken up when other forms of conflict resolution have been exhausted."[10] In every respect—ideologically, strategically, and organizationally—military capacity, while necessary, must always remain secondary to the political project. Perhaps the most important element of "Liberatory Community Armed Self-Defense" is *community*. (*Armed* should be the least important.) However liberatory the ideology motivating it, to the degree that the group bearing arms understands itself as a distinct and separate entity, there are likely to be problems—elitism, vanguardism, authoritarianism, machismo, and the myriad ills they produce.

When I asked him to reflect on these ideas a few years after his book *Setting Sights* appeared, scott crow was frank about the challenges involved in organizing with the capacity for violence without creating hierarchies based on violence.[11] It can't only consist of the standard gun training but with an anti-oppression workshop added on. At its most basic, there must be a concerted effort to "mak[e] sure that the most marginalized [people] have access to the tools [of violence] and also have the support to learn to use them." But that process itself needs to extend beyond patronizing liberal notions of diversity and inclusion to emphasize instead "building longer-term trust and relationships"—not only within the armed grouping but also between its members and the larger communities. Clearly not everyone needs to (or should) engage in the armed or militant aspects of the struggle, but those who take on that role need to be authentically integrated into and accountable to the community they are defending and on whose behalf they act. "Defending the community is not service work," crow insists. "It's part of liberatory mutual aid."

This collectivist understanding, concomitant with the liberatory objectives, helps to distinguish *community defense* from the idea of *self-defense* implicit in the mainstream gun culture and re-layed (for example) in the standard NRA training. That "attitude of defense . . . isolates you from the rest of civil society," crow ex-plains, "because it's all about how you and your family are going to survive the apocalypse. . . . It doesn't enculturate cooperation and resource-sharing. It incorporates cultures of fear and isolation." Ultimately, he says, it "reinforces the worst of white male patri-archy, and the state." Community defense, in contrast, requires a break from our society's typical assumptions about who has the right to bear arms (historically, white citizens), who enjoys a mon-opoly on violence (the state and its auxiliaries), and the centrality of violence to masculinity (and vice versa). It is not merely a ques-tion of who has firearms, or even who has power, but of how we conceive of power and how we organize—and constrain—violence.

Toward a Less Violent World

A genuinely anarchist society would likely be, on the whole, paci-fist. If we want to eliminate coercion from our social relations, it follows that the role of violence—personal or institutional—would be reduced to infinitesimal levels and likely condemned (or at least regretted) when it does occur. However, to build *that* world, we must act in *this* world. The process of change will sometimes en-tail violence, if only to protect peaceable people from police raids and death squads. This introduces an irresolvable paradox: the means required to build a just society may not be suited to that society. Unfortunately, we cannot rely on practices that are purely prefigurative, that encompass in themselves the values they seek to advance; but neither can we surrender those values in the course of struggle and expect to find them waiting for us, fully realized, "after the revolution."

Violence should, I think, always be understood as morally compromising and politically problematic, as well as physically dangerous and psychologically damaging—even when absolutely necessary. It should therefore only be organized with the utmost care, not only for the technical and the tactical aspects but also with attention to the various impacts it may have on individuals, communities, and the social movement. We must be careful that the organizations we build do not become impediments to the society we wish to create. The available means will always be imperfect; that is a fact we must accept. The means we adopt should not, however, render our ends unattainable. In matters of revolutionary organization, cynicism can be as impractical as utopianism and infinitely more corrupting.

Acknowledgments

The three essays comprising the bulk of this book were composed over the course of many years, and my thinking in that time has benefited from any number of conversations, with a wide variety of scholars, activists, and everyday people. I am grateful to all those who have taken the time to share their insights and the lessons of their experience with me.

Special thanks to those who offered criticism and comments on one or more of these essays as I drafted and revised them: Effie Baum, Jules Boykoff, Luis Brennan, Shane Burley, Amelia Caites, George Ciccariello-Maher, scott crow, Emily-Jane Dawson, Colette Gordon, Don Hamerquist, Chris Knudtsen, Eric Laursen, Peter Little, Geoff McNamara, Will Munger, Steve Niva, Janeen P., Gabriel Ryder, Josef Schneider, Spencer Sunshine, M. Treloar, Kevin Van Meter, Lesley Wood, and Xtn.

Notes

Questioning Under Caution: An Introductory Note

1. Nicholas Abercrombie, Stephen Hill, and Bryan S. Turner, eds., *Penguin Dictionary of Sociology*, 4th ed. (London: Penguin Books, 2000), s.v. "Gang," 147–48.
2. Quoted in Shannon E. Reid and Matthew Valasik, *Alt-Right Gangs: A Hazy Shade of White* (Oakland: University of California Press, 2020), 6.
3. "About Violent Gangs," U.S. Department of Justice, April 30, 2021, https://www.justice.gov/criminal-ocgs/about-violent-gangs.
4. Both the *Penguin Dictionary of Sociology* and *Alt-Right Gangs* refer to the controversies attached to any definition. Abercrombie, Hill, and Turner, *Penguin Dictionary of Sociology*, 4th ed., 148; and, Reid and Valasik, *Alt-Right Gangs*, 3–6. If pressed, we could follow something like the procedure I employed when defining "police" in *Our Enemies in Blue* and assemble the above criteria to construct an ideal type. To the degree that a particular organization matched the criteria, we could say with certainty that it would qualify. This approach may be thought of as more diagnostic than definitional. Rather than a strict yes-no binary, it would allow us to position different groups along a spectrum as being *more* gang-like or *less*. Kristian Williams, *Our Enemies in Blue: Police and Power in America*, 3rd ed. (Oakland: AK Press, 2015), 51–55.
5. I wrote in *Our Enemies in Blue*: "By 'crime' I do not mean mere illegality, but instead a category of socially proscribed acts that: (1) threaten or harm other people and (2) violate norms related to justice, personal safety, or human rights, (3) in such a manner or to such a degree as to warrant community intervention (and sometimes coercive intervention). That category

would surely include a large number of things that are presently illegal (rape, murder, dropping bricks off an overpass), would certainly *not* include other things that are presently illegal (smoking pot, sleeping in public parks, nude sunbathing), and would likely *also* include some things that are *not* presently illegal (mass evictions, the invasion of Iraq)." Williams, *Our Enemies in Blue*, 365.

The Other Side of the Coin:
Counterinsurgency and Community Policing

This chapter first appeared as Kristian Williams, "The Other Side of the COIN: Counterinsurgency and Community Policing," *Interface: A Journal for and about Social Movements* 3 no. 1 (May 2011). A different version was included in Kristian Williams, Lara Messersmith-Glavin, and Will Munger, eds., *Life during Wartime: Resisting Counterinsurgency* (Oakland: AK Press, 2013). The present iteration has been edited and updated for this volume, emphasizing its relevance to gangs and restoring some of the military theory from the original.

1. Quoted in Laura Trevelyan, "Bill Bratton to Advise at UK Gang Conference," BBC News, October 9, 2011, http://www.bbc.co.uk/news/uk-15229199.

2. U.S. Army, *Counterinsurgency*, Field Manual 3-24 (Washington, DC: Dept. of the Army, 2006), 1-2.

3. U.S. Army, *Counterinsurgency*, 1‒113.

4. U.S. Army, 1‒123.

5. Justin Gage, William Martin, Tim Mitchell, and Pat Wingate, *Winning the Peace in Iraq: Confronting America's Informational and Doctrinal Handicaps* (Norfolk, VA: Joint Forces Staff College, Joint Combined Warfighting School, 2003), 1.

6. David Petraeus, quoted in "General Says Iraq Talks Critical," BBC News, March 8, 2007, http://news.bbc.co.uk/2/hi/6429519.stm.

7. David C. Gompert and John Gordon IV, et al., *War by Other Means: Building Complete and Balanced Capabilities for Counterinsurgency* (Santa Monica: RAND, 2008), 76.

8. Michel Foucault, *"Society Must Be Defended": Lectures at the Collège de France, 1975‒76*, eds. Mauro Bertani and Alessandro Fontana, trans. David Macey (New York: Picador, 2003), 15‒16.

9. Max Weber, "The Profession and Vocation of Politics," in *Political Writings*, eds. Peter Lassman and Ronald Speirs (Cambridge: Cambridge University Press, 2005), 310‒11.

10. "Liberal": Hugo Slim, *With or Against? Humanitarian Agencies and Coalition Counter-Insurgency* (n.p.: Centre for Humanitarian Dialogue, 2004), 3. "Radical": Sarah Sewall, "Introduction to the University of Chicago Press Edition: A Radical Field Manual," in U.S., Department of the Army, *The U.S. Army/ Marine Corps Counterinsurgency Field Manual: U.S. Army Field Manual No. 3-24; Marine Corps Warfighting Publication No. 3-33.5* (Chicago: University of Chicago Press, 2007), xxi.

11. U.S. Army, *Counterinsurgency*, 1-113, 1-115.

12. Gompert and Gordon, *War by Other Means*, xxxvii.

13. U.S. Army, *Counterinsurgency*, 3-2.

14. To help answer these questions, the Pentagon invested $50 million to recruit social scientists to serve as analysts in its "Minerva Program." Hugh Gusterson, "Militarizing Knowledge," in *The Counter-Counterinsurgency Manual: Or, Notes on Demilitarizing American Society*, ed. Network of Concerned Anthropologists Steering Committee (Chicago: Prickly Paradigm Press, 2009), 51.

15. U.S. Army, *Counterinsurgency*, B-47.

16. U.S. Army, B-49.

17. Martin C. Libicki, et al., *Byting Back: Regaining Information Superiority against 21st-Century Insurgents* (Santa Monica: RAND, 2007), 21.

18. Libicki, *Byting Back*, 133.

19. Libicki, 21–23.

20. For my full account of the relationship between militarization and community policing, see Kristian Williams, "Your Friendly Neighborhood Police State," chap. 9 in *Our Enemies in Blue: Police and Power in America*, 3rd ed. (Oakland: AK Press, 2015). The quote appears on page 353.

21. Gompert and Gordon, *War by Other Means*, xlv.

22. Joseph D. Celeski, *Policing and Law Enforcement in COIN: Thick Blue Line* (Hulburt Field, FL: JSOU Press, 2009), 40. On pseudo-operations, see Frank Kitson, *Gangs and Counter-Gangs* (London: Barrie and Rockliff, 1960).

23. William Rosenau, *Subversion and Insurgency* (Santa Monica: RAND, 2007), 15.

24. Austin Long, *On Other War: Lessons from Five Decades of RAND Counterinsurgency Research* (Santa Monica: RAND, 2006), 53.

25. Center for Research on Criminal Justice, *The Iron Fist and the Velvet Glove: An Analysis of the U.S. Police* (Berkeley: Center for Research on Criminal Justice, 1975), 48–50.

26. Clark McPhail, David Schweingruber, and John McCarthy, "Policing Protest in the United States: 1960–1995," chap. 2 in *Policing Protest: The Control of Mass Demonstrations in Western Democracies*, eds. Donnatella Della Porta and Herbert Reiter (Minneapolis: University of Minnesota Press, 1998).

27. Daryl F. Gates with Diane K. Shah, *Chief: My Life in the LAPD* (New York:

Bantam Books, 1992), 109; and Ken Lawrence, *The New State Repression* (Portland, Ore.: Tarantula, 2006), 13–16.

28. Center for Research on Criminal Justice, *The Iron Fist and the Velvet Glove*, 30.

29. Jason H. Beers, *Community-Oriented Policing and Counterinsurgency: A Conceptual Model* (Fort Leavenworth, KS: U.S. Army Command and General Staff College, 2007), 77.

30. Celeski, *Policing and Law Enforcement in COIN*, 43; Libicki, *Byting Back*, 79–80; and, Gary D. Calese, *Law Enforcement Methods for Counterinsurgency Operations* (Fort Leavenworth, KS.: U.S. Army Command and General Staff College, School of Advanced Military Studies, 2004), 41–42.

31. Libicki, *Byting Back*, 25.

32. Sidney L. Harring and Gerda W. Ray, "Policing a Class Society: New York City in the 1990s," *Social Justice*, 26, no. 2 (Summer 1999).

33. Christian Parenti, *Lockdown America: Police and Prisons in the Age of Crisis* (London: Verso, 1999), 75–76, 83–89.

34. Siobhan Gorman, "LAPD Terror-Tip Plan May Serve as Model," *Wall Street Journal*, April 15, 2008; Josh Meyer, "LAPD Leads the Way in Local Counter-Terrorism," *Los Angeles Times*, April 14, 2008; Michael German and Jay Stanley, *What's Wrong with Fusion Centers?* (New York: American Civil Liberties Union, 2007); and, Mike German and Jay Stanley, *Fusion Center Update* (New York: American Civil Liberties Union, 2008).

35. Conor Friedersdorf, "The Surveillance City of Camden, New Jersey," *Atlantic*, December 12, 2013, https://www.theatlantic.com/national/archive/2013/12/the-surveillance-city-of-camden-new-jersey/282286.

36. Matt Taibbi, "Apocalypse, New Jersey: A Dispatch from America's Most Desperate Town," *Rolling Stone*, December 11, 2013, https://www.rollingstone.com/culture/culture-news/apocalypse-new-jersey-a-dispatch-from-americas-most-desperate-town-56174; and Brendan McQuade, "The Demilitarization Ruse," *Jacobin*, May 24, 2015, https://www.jacobinmag.com/2015/05/camden-obama-police-brutality-black-lives-matter.

37. McKenna also said, "Jihad, Crips, extreme animal-rights activists, it's all the same: people trying damage the system." Both quotes from Judy Peet, "NJIT Homeland Security Center Studies Groundbreaking Anti-Terrorism Technology," *NJ.com*, June 12, 2010, https://www.nj.com/news/2010/06/njit_scientists_homeland_secur.html.

38. Lynette Clemetson, "Homeland Security Given Data on Arab-Americans," *New York Times*, July 30, 2004.

39. Quoted in Michael Isikoff, "The FBI Says, Count the Mosques," *Newsweek*, February 3, 2003, https://www.newsweek.com/investigators-fbi-says-count-mosques-140311.

40. American Civil Liberties Union, "ACLU Calls FBI Mosque-Counting Scheme

Blatant Ethnic and Religious Profiling," press release, January 27, 2003, https://www.aclu.org/press-releases/aclu-calls-fbi-mosque-counting-scheme -blatant-ethnic-and-religious-profiling.

41. Philip Heymann, "Muslims in America After 9/11: The Legal Situation," in *Muslims in Europe and the United States: A Transatlantic Comparison* (Cambridge, MA: Minda de Gunzburg Center for European Studies at Harvard University, 2006), http://www.ces.fas.harvard.edu/conferences/muslims/Heymann .pdf.

42. Jerry Markon, "Tension Grows between Calif. Muslims, FBI after Informant Infiltrates Mosque," *Washington Post*, December 5, 2010.

43. Richard Winton, Teresa Watanabe, and Greg Krikorian, "LAPD Defends Muslim Mapping Effort," *Los Angeles Times*, November 10, 2007.

44. Quoted in Winton, "LAPD Defends Muslim Mapping Effort."

45. Quoted in Matt Apuzzo and Adam Goldman, "With CIA Help, NYPD Moves Covertly in Muslim Areas," Associated Press Archive, August 25, 2011. For a short history of the "human terrain" idea, see Roberto González, *American Counterinsurgency: Human Science and the Human Terrain* (Chicago: Prickly Paradigm, 2009), especially chap. 2, "The Origins of Human Terrain."

46. George L. Kelling and William J. Bratton, "Policing Terrorism," *Civic Bulletin*, September 2006, https://www.manhattan-institute.org/html/policing-terrorism-5636.html. The Manhattan Institute proudly describes itself as "an important force in shaping American political culture and developing ideas that foster economic choice and individual responsibility," adding, "our work has won new respect for market-oriented policies and helped make reform a reality." "About the Manhattan Institute," Manhattan Institute, http://www.manhattan-institute.org/html/about_mi_30.htm, accessed February 6, 2012.

47. James Q. Wilson and George L. Kelling, "Broken Windows," *Atlantic Monthly*, March 1982.

48. Kelling and Bratton, "Policing Terrorism," 2.

49. Kelling and Bratton, 4.

50. Kelling and Bratton, 5. The authors do offer a pro forma caution: "We also need to be mindful of the mess that local police departments got themselves into in the 1960s by illegally spying on antiwar and civil rights groups. Uniform training procedures and standards on how intelligence is gathered, stored, and accessed need to be developed and disseminated to local law enforcement in order to safeguard citizens' privacy and civil rights." Kelling and Bratton, 5.

51. Kelling and Bratton, 6.

52. Kelling and Bratton, 3.

53. Kelling and Bratton, 4.

54. Kelling and Bratton, 4–5.

55. Julie Watson, "Cops Show Marines How to Take on the Taliban," *NBC Los Angeles*, July 12, 2010, http://www.nbclosangeles.com/news/local-beat/Cops -Show-Marines-How-to-Take-on-the-Taliban-98202989.html.

56. Elisabeth Bumiller, "U.S. Tries to Reintegrate Taliban Soldiers," *New York Times*, May 23, 2010.

57. For a detailed discussion of the Salinas partnership, see Will Munger, "Social War in the Salad Bowl," in *Life during Wartime: Resisting Counterinsurgency*, eds. Kristian Williams, Lara Messersmith-Glavin, and Will Munger (Oakland: AK Press, 2013).

58. Karl Vick, "Iraq's Lessons, On the Home Front," *Washington Post*, November 15, 2009.

59. Louis Fetherolf, *90-Day Report to the Community* (Salinas, Calif.: Salinas Police Department, 2009), 15–16.

60. According to the police chief, the youth programs provided "more youth in the community alternatives to gang lifestyles and in the process develop[ed] a growing pool of home-grown, future police officers." Louis Fetherolf, *180-Day Report to the Community* (Salinas, CA: Salinas Police Department, October 20, 2009), 33–34. One officer-instructor explained the benefits of the parenting classes: "The parent participants who have applied what they learned have seen dramatic positive changes in their homes . . . and these classes have helped to grow police legitimacy." *Evaluation of Strategic Work Plan: Salinas Comprehensive Strategy for Community-Wide Violence Reduction* (Oakland: National Council on Crime and Delinquency, 2015), 17.

61. Quoted in Munger, "Social War in the Salad Bowl," 119–20. By 2014, "nearly 70 organizations and leaders, including 14 individuals, 41 CBOs [community-based organizations], four city departments, and eight county departments" had joined the Community Alliance for Safety and Peace (CASP), "with approximately 45 of these being active members (e.g., regularly attending CASP meetings)." *Evaluation of Strategic Work Plan*, 6.

62. Munger, "Social War in the Salad Bowl," 115–24.

63. *Evaluation of Strategic Work Plan*, 7.

64. *Evaluation of Strategic Work Plan*, 14.

65. Fetherolf, *180-Day Report to the Community*.

66. Julia Reynolds, "Operation Knockout: Gang Raid Targets Nuestra Familia in Salinas," *Monterey Herald*, April 23, 2010.

67. Quoted in Julia Reynolds, "After Operation Knockout, Salinas Police Focus on Prevention," *Monterey Herald*, April 24, 2010.

68. *Evaluation of Strategic Work Plan*, 9.

69. *Evaluation of Strategic Work Plan*, 4.

70. *Evaluation of Strategic Work Plan*, 19.

71. *Evaluation of Strategic Work Plan*, 22.

72. *Evaluation of Strategic Work Plan*, 28, 26.

73. One participant complained, "Conversations in CASP are controlled by people in power." A nonparticipant likewise observed, "CASP has mostly people from government." She then went on to suggest that the group was too tied to business interests: "They are really about building more money instead of about communities." Both quoted in *Evaluation of Strategic Work Plan*, 29.

74. *Evaluation of Strategic Work Plan*, 30.

75. Roberto Santos, et al., *Collaborative Reform Initiative: An Assessment of the Salinas Police Department* (Washington, DC: U.S. Department of Justice, Office of Community Oriented Policing Services, 2016), 1.

76. Santos, *Collaborative Reform Initiative*, 9.

77. Santos, 34–35, 37–48, 67, 70–72, and 116–19.

78. Santos, 4. See also page 80.

79. Santos, 81.

80. Santos, 79.

81. David M. Kennedy, Anthony A. Braga, and Anne M. Piehl, "Developing and Implementing Operation Ceasefire," in Anthony A. Braga and David M. Kennedy, *Reducing Gun Violence: The Boston Gun Project's Operation Ceasefire* (Washington, DC: U.S. Department of Justice, National Institute of Justice, 2001), 5–53; Anthony A. Braga and Christopher Winship, "Creating an Effective Foundation to Prevent Youth Violence: Lessons from Boston in the 1990s," *Rappaport Institute for Greater Boston Policy Briefs*, September 26, 2005; and "Reducing Gang Violence in Boston," chap. 9 in *Responding to Gangs: Evaluation and Research*, eds. Winifred L. Reed and Scott H. Decker (Washington, DC: U.S. Department of Justice, Office of Justice Programs, National Institute of Justice, 2002).

82. Kennedy, Braga, and Piehl, "Developing and Implementing Operation Ceasefire"; and David M. Kennedy, Anthony A. Braga, and Anne M. Piehl, "The (Un)Known Universe: Mapping Gangs and Gang Violence in Boston," chap. 8 in *Crime Mapping and Crime Prevention*, eds. David Weisburd and Tom McEwen (Monsey, N.Y.: Criminal Justice Press, 1997).

83. David Kennedy, "Pulling Levers: Getting Deterrence Right," *National Institute of Justice Journal*, no. 236 (July 1998): 5.

84. Braga and Winship, "Creating an Effective Foundation to Prevent Youth Violence"; Kennedy, Braga, and Piehl, "Developing and Implementing Operation Ceasefire"; and "Reducing Gang Violence in Boston."

85. Kennedy, "Pulling Levers," 6.

86. Jean M. McGloin, *Street Gangs and Interventions: Innovative Problem Solving with Network Analysis* (Washington, DC: U.S. Department of Justice, Office of Community Oriented Policing Services, 2005), 9–13.

87. McGloin, *Street Gangs and Interventions*, 14–18.

88. McGloin, 18.

89. Gompert and Gordon, *War by Other Means*, 25.

90. Braga and Winship, "Creating an Effective Foundation to Prevent Youth Violence," 6.

91. Gompert and Gordon, *War by Other Means*, 25.

92. Community Capacity Development Office, *Weed and Seed Implementation Manual* (Washington, DC: U.S. Department of Justice, 2005), 1.

93. U.S. Army, *Counterinsurgency*, 5-50, 5-51.

94. U.S. Army, 5-70.

95. Quoted in Peter B. Kraska and Victor E. Kappeler, "Militarizing American Police: The Rise and Normalization of Paramilitary Units," in *The Police and Society: Touchstone Readings*, ed. Victor E. Kappeler (Prospect Heights, IL/: Waveland Press, 1999), 473.

96. Quoted in Dick Lilly, "City Urged to Bury Weed and Seed Plan," *Seattle Times*, March 27, 1992.

97. Salinas Police Department, "Operation Ceasefire and Operation Knock-out," *Report to the Community*, July 2010, 4.

98. Scott Kraft, "A City's Enemy Within," *Los Angeles Times*, June 16, 2010.

99. Joseph E. Long, *Social Movement Theory Typology of Gang Violence* (master's thesis, Naval Postgraduate School, Dept. of Defense Analysis, 2010), 35-77.

100. Quoted in Parenti, *Lockdown America*, 111, emphasis added.

101. Judith Greene and Kevin Pranis, *Gang Wars: The Failure of Enforcement Tactics and the Need for Effective Public Safety Strategies* (Washington, DC: Justice Policy Institute, 2007), 6.

102. Critical Resistance Oakland, *Betraying the Model City: How Gang Injunctions Fail Oakland* (Oakland: Critical Resistance, 2011); and Frank P. Barajas, "An Invading Army: A Civil Gang Injunction in a Southern California Chicana/o Community," *Latino Studies*, 5, no. 4 (2007). For more on gang injunctions, see Stop the Injunctions Coalition, "Our Oakland, Our Solutions," in *Life during Wartime: Resisting Counterinsurgency,* eds. Kristian Williams, Lara Messersmith-Glavin, and Will Munger (Oakland: AK Press, 2013).

103. Felix M. Padilla, *Gangs as an American Enterprise* (New Brunswick, NJ: Rutgers University Press, 1992), 85; and Randall G. Sheldon, Sharon K. Tracy, and William B. Brown, *Youth Gangs in American Society*, 2nd ed. (Belmont, CA: Wandsworth, 2001), 244.

104. Mike Davis, "L.A.: The Fire This Time," *CovertAction Information Bulletin*, no. 41 (Summer 1992): 115-16; Malcolm W. Klein, *The American Street Gang: Its Nature, Prevalence, and Control* (New York: Oxford University Press, 1995); and Irving A. Spergel, *The Youth Gang Problem: A Community Approach* (New York: Oxford University Press, 1995), 191.

105. Davis, "L.A.: The Fire This Time," 18.

106. "Institutionalization . . . is composed of three main components: First, the *routinization* of collective action. . . . Second, *inclusion* and *marginalization*,

whereby challengers who are willing to adhere to established routines will be granted access to political exchanges in mainstream institutions, while those who refuse to accept them can be shut out of conversations through either repression or neglect. Third, *cooptation*, which means that challengers alter their claims and tactics to ones that can be pursued without disrupting the normal practice of politics." David S. Meyer and Sidney Tarrow, "A Movement Society: Contentious Politics for a New Century," in *The Social Movement Society: Contentious Politics for a New Century*, eds. David S. Meyer and Sidney Tarrow (Lanham, MD: Rowman and Littlefield, 1998), 21.

107. Daniel Byman, *Understanding Proto-Insurgencies* (Santa Monica: RAND, 2007), 24.

108. *Evaluation of Strategic Work Plan*, 17.

109. U.S. Army, *Counterinsurgency*, 1-153, emphasis in original.

110. For example: Arundhati Roy, "Public Power in the Age of Empire," *Democracy Now*, August 23, 2004, http://www.democracynow.org/2004/8/23/public _power_in_the_age_of#; Ji Giles Ungpakorn, "NGOs: Enemies or Allies," *International Socialism,* no. 104 (October 2004), http://isj.org.uk/ngos-enemies -or-allies; Yves Engler, "Occupation by NGO," *CounterPunch*, August 13–15, 2010, https://www.counterpunch.org/2010/08/13/occupation-by-ngo; and James Petras, "NGOs: In the Service of Imperialism," *Journal of Contemporary Asia*, 29 no. 4, 1999.

111. Colin Powell, "Remarks to the National Foreign Policy Conference for Leaders of Nongovernmental Organizations," October 26, 2001, Avalon Project: Documents in Law, History and Diplomacy, Yale Law School, http://avalon.law.yale.edu/sept11/powell_brief31.asp.

112. Quoted in "Guidelines for NGHO–U.S. Military Relations," *Small Wars Journal*, July 30, 2007, https://smallwarsjournal.com/blog/guidelines-for -ngho-us-military-relations.

113. U.S. Army, *Counterinsurgency*, 1-122.

114. John Arquilla and David Ronfeldt, "Summary," in *Networks and Netwars: The Future of Terror, Crime, and Militancy* (Santa Monica: RAND, 2001), x.

115. GRAIN, *The Soils of War: The Real Agenda Behind Agricultural Reconstruction in Afghanistan and Iraq*, March 2009, http://www.grain.org/briefings/?id=217.

116. Quoted in David Rieff, "How NGOs Became Pawns in the War on Terrorism," *New Republic*, August 3, 2010, https://newrepublic.com/article/76752/war -terrorism-ngo-perversion.

117. Greg Miller and Peter Finn, "CIA Sees Increased Threat from al-Qaeda in Yemen," *Washington Post*, August 24, 2010; and Andrew Y. Zelin, "What if Obama's Yemen Policy Works?," *Middle East Channel*, September 22, 2010, http://mideast.foreignpolicy.com/posts/2010/09/22/what_if _obama_s_yemen_policy_works.

118. Quoted in Robert E. Mitchell, "Yemen: Testing a New Coordinated Approach to Preventive Counterinsurgency," *Small Wars Journal*, August 1, 2011, https://smallwarsjournal.com/blog/journal/docs-temp/826-mitchell.pdf.

119. Jeremy M. Sharp, *Yemen: Background and U.S. Relations* (Washington, DC: Congressional Research Service, October 6, 2011); Mark Mazzetti, "U.S. Is Intensifying a Secret Campaign of Yemen Airstrikes," *New York Times*, June 8, 2011; and "Jeremy Scahill: As Mass Uprising Threatens the Saleh Regime, a Look at the Covert U.S. War in Yemen," *Democracy Now*, March 22, 2011, http://www.democracynow.org/2011/3/22/jeremy _scahill_as_mass_uprising_threatens.

120. Mitchell, "Yemen."

121. Rieff, "How NGOs Became Pawns in the War on Terrorism."

122. Operation Ceasefire quotation: Braga and Winship, "Creating an Effective Foundation to Prevent Youth Violence," 4–5.

123. George Ciccariello-Maher, "Oakland's Not for Burning? Popular Fury at Yet Another Police Murder," *CounterPunch*, January 9–11, 2009, https:// www.counterpunch.org/2009/01/09/oakland-s-not-for-burning.

124. Quoted in George Ciccariello-Maher, "'Oakland Is Closed!': Arrest and Containment Fail to Blunt Anger in the Streets," *CounterPunch*, January 16–18, 2009, https://www.counterpunch.org/2009/01/16/quot-oakland-is-closed -quot.

125. George Ciccariello-Maher, "From Arizona to Oakland: The Intersections of Mass Work and Revolutionary Politics," Bring the Ruckus panel discussion, Portland, Oregon October 23, 2010.

126. Ciccariello-Maher, "Oakland Is Closed!"

127. Ciccariello-Maher, "Oakland Is Closed!"; and Advance the Struggle, *Justice for Oscar Grant: A Lost Opportunity?* ([Oakland]: 2009), https://libcom.org/ library/justice-oscar-grant-lost-opportunity.

128. Raider Nation Collective, introduction to *Raider Nation*, vol. 1, *From the January Rebellions to Lovelle Mixon and Beyond* (Oakland: Raider Nation Collective, 2010); and George Ciccariello-Maher, "'Fired Up, Can't Take It No More': From Oakland to Santa Rita, the Struggle Continues," *CounterPunch*, February 3, 2009, https://www.counterpunch.org/2009/02/03/quot -fired-up-can-t-take-it-no-more-quot.

129. Ali Winston, "Anarchists, the FBI and the Aftermath of the Oscar Grant Murder Trial," *Informant*, January 27, 2011, http://informant.kalwnews.org /2011/01/anarchists-the-fbi-and-the-aftermath-of-the-oscar-grant-murder -trial/#more-5247; Ali Winston, "L.A. Oscar Grant Protests Also Monitored by Law Enforcement," *Informant*, January 6, 2011, http://informant .kalwnews.org/2011/01/la-oscar-grant-protests-also-monitored-by-law -enforcement/#more-4592; Ali Winston, "Logs Detail Oakland Police Surveillance of Grant Protestors, Concerns about 'Anarchists,'" *Infor-*

mant, January 7, 2011, http://informant.kalwnews.org/2011/01/logs-detail -oakland-police-surveillance-of-grant-protesters-concerns-about-anarchists; Ali Winston, "Monitoring Protests: Normal Policing or Something Deeper?," *Informant*, December 16, 2010, http://informant.kalwnews.org /2010/12/monitoring-the-oscar-grant-protests-normal-policing-or-something -deeper; and Ali Winston, "Police Files Reveal Interest in Oscar Grant Protests, 'Anarchists,'" *Informant*, December 15, 2010, http://informant.kalwnews .org/2010/12/police-documents-reveal-federal-interest-in-oscar-grant-pro tests-anarchists.

130. Ciccariello-Maher, "From Arizona to Oakland."

131. Nicole Lee, "Bracing for Mehserle Verdict: Community Engagement Plan," in *Advance the Struggle*, June 27, 2010, http://advancethestruggle.wordpress .com. Emphasis in original.

132. Raider Nation Collective, "Lessons Never Learned: Nonprofits and the State, Redux," *Bay Area Independent Media Center*, June 30, 2010, https:// www.indybay.org/newsitems/2010/06/30/18652347.php.

133. Youth UpRising, "Violence Is Not Justice," YouTube.com, July 6, 2010, http://www.youtube.com/watch?v=XqofgXqteuQ. The organization's website, YouthUprising.org, later quoted Attorney General Eric Holder saying the group was a "perfect example of what we need to be doing around the country." Quoted in YouthUprising.org, viewed October 14, 2010.

134. George Ciccariello-Maher, "Chronicle of a Riot Foretold," *Counter-Punch*, June 29, 2010, https://www.counterpunch.org/2010/06/29/chronicle -of-a-riot-foretold.

135. Ciccariello-Maher, "Chronicle of a Riot Foretold."

136. George Ciccariello-Maher, "Oakland's Verdict," *CounterPunch*, July 12, 2010, https://www.counterpunch.org/2010/07/12/oakland-s-verdict.

137. A few months later, radicals in Seattle reported a similar dynamic, co-opted community leaders suppressing unrest after police killed a Native American man. Nightwolf and Mamos, "How Can We Advance the Anti-Police Brutality Struggle?" *Gathering Forces*, December 24, 2010, https://web .archive.org/web/20101230105424/http://gatheringforces.org/2010/12/24/how -can-we-advance-the-anti-police-brutality-struggle.

138. Advance the Struggle, *Justice for Oscar Grant*, 8–9. For similar critiques of the role nonprofits play in managing political struggle, see Incite! Women of Color Against Violence, ed., *The Revolution Will Not Be Funded: Beyond the Non-Profit Industrial Complex* (Cambridge, MA: South End Press, 2007).

139. Advance the Struggle, *Justice for Oscar Grant*, 22. The cop who shot Grigoropoulos was convicted and sentenced to life in prison. Associated Press, "Greece: Police Officer Convicted in Killing That Led to Riots," *New York Times*, October 11, 2010.

Gangs, States, and Insurgencies

This essay began as a lecture: Kristian Williams, "Gang Suppression as Counterinsurgency," John F. Kennedy Institute for North American Studies, Freie Universität Berlin: Berlin, Germany, January 21, 2016. The audience was the "Gang Suppression in the Americas" class of professors Markus-Michael Müller and Markus Kienscherf.

1 Baynard Woods, "Can a Truce between Baltimore's Gangs Help Make the City Safer?," *Baltimore City Paper*, May 5, 2015, https://www.baltimoresun .com/citypaper/bcpnews-can-a-truce-between-baltimores-gangs-help-make -the-city-safer-20150505-story.html. Reports conflict as to whether there was a general prohibition on attacking businesses or only Black-owned businesses. Suzy Khimm, "We're Going to Protect Our Community Ourselves," *New Republic*, May 3, 2015, https://newrepublic.com/article/121703/ baltimore-gang-truce-over-freddie-gray-can-it-last.

2. Khimm, "We're Going to Protect Our Community Ourselves." As one gang leader told the *City Paper*, his set had been busy "protecting the businesses and making sure no one [was] going into those stores. A lot of products taken out of those stores, we actually took back. And we put them behind us and we formed a line around the stores and the property and stuff." Quoted in Woods, "Can a Truce between Baltimore's Gangs Help."

3. Baltimore Police Department Media Relations Section, "Credible Threat to Law Enforcement," press release, April 27, 2015, Maryland Troopers Association, https://mdtroopers.org/general/credible-threat-to-law-enforcement. Emphasis in original.

4. Christopher Mathias, "Baltimore Gang Members Say They Never Formed Truce to Hurt Cops," *Huffington Post*, April 28, 2015, https://www.huffpost.com /entry/baltimore-gangs-cops-freddie-gray_n_7162350; Woods, "Can a Truce Between Baltimore's Gangs Help"; and Khimm, "We're Going to Protect Our Community Ourselves."

5. Woods, "Can a Truce Between Baltimore's Gangs Help."

6. Brian Charles, "Baltimore Gangs Agree to Truce Similar to One During 1992 Riots in L.A.," *Los Angeles Daily News*, April 30, 2015.

7. Quoted in Woods, "Can a Truce Between Baltimore's Gangs Help."

8. Quoted in Baynard Woods, "Baltimore's Uprising: Rival Gangs Push for Peace after Freddie Gray's Death," *Guardian*, April 27, 2016.

9. See Kristian Williams, "The Other Side of the COIN: Counterinsurgency and Community Policing," in this volume.

10. Max G. Manwaring, *Street Gangs: The New Urban Insurgency* (Carlisle, PA: Strategic Studies Institute, 2005); Joseph E. Long, "Social Movement Theory Typology of Gang Violence" (master's thesis, Naval Postgraduate

School, Dept. of Defense Analysis, 2010); John P. Sullivan, "Future Conflict: Criminal Insurgencies, Gangs and Intelligence," *Small Wars Journal*, May 31, 2009, https://smallwarsjournal.com/jrnl/art/future-conflict-criminal-insurgencies-gangs-and-intelligence; John P. Sullivan, "Gangs, Hooligans, and Anarchists: The Vanguard of Netwar in the Streets," chap. 4 in *Networks and Netwars: The Future of Terror, Crime, and Militancy*, eds. John Arquilla and David Ronfeldt (Santa Monica: RAND, 2001); Joint Chiefs of Staff, "Appendix A: Insurgency and Crime," in *Counterinsurgency Operations*, Joint Publication 3-24 (Washington, DC: Joint Chiefs of Staff, 2009); and Darren E. Tromblay, "America's Unacknowledged Insurgency: Addressing Street Gangs as Threats to National Security," *Small Wars Journal*, February 6, 2016, https://smallwarsjournal.com/jrnl/art/america%E2%80%99s-unacknowledged-insurgency-addressing-street-gangs-as-threats-to-national-security. Darren Tromblay, a U.S. government intelligence analyst, writes: "The problem that U.S. street gangs pose is a direct challenge to U.S. sovereignty. The use of violence and direct challenge to legitimate authorities is, by itself, a threat to security no different than the wanton violence of a group such as the Islamic State." Indicative of his sense of proportion, he also advocates "Serious consideration . . . [as] to whether associated cultural accouterments such as 'gangster rap' constitute sedition." Tromblay, "America's Unacknowledged Insurgency," *Small Wars Journal*.

11. Sullivan, "Gangs, Hooligans, and Anarchists," 102.

12. Sullivan, 113–14.

13. Mike Davis, *City of Quartz: Excavating the Future in Los Angeles* (New York: Vintage Books, 1992), 293. For a good overview of this history, see Alex A. Alonso, "Racialized Identities and the Formation of Black Gangs in Los Angeles," *Urban Geography*, no. 25 (2004). For a more general history, including comparisons with other cities, see James C. Howell and John P. Moore, "History of Street Gangs in the United States," *National Gang Center Bulletin* (U.S. Department of Justice, Bureau of Justice Assistance), May 2010.

14. Tom Hayden, *Street Wars: Gangs and the Future of Violence* (New York: New Press, 2004), 166–67.

15. Hayden, *Street Wars*, 160–63; Davis, *City of Quartz*, 297; Judson L. Jeffries and Malcolm Foley, "To Live and Die in L.A.," in *Comrades: A Local History of the Black Panther Party*, ed. Judson L. Jeffries (Bloomington: Indiana University Press, 2007), 261; Akinyele O. Umoja, "The Black Liberation Army and the Radical Legacy of the Black Panther Party," in *Black Power in the Belly of the Beast* (Urbana: University of Illinois Press, 2006), 227–28; and Joshua Bloom and Waldo E. Martin Jr., *Black against Empire: The History of the Black Panther Party* (Oakland: University of California Press, 2013), 144.

16. Bloom and Martin, *Black against Empire*, 291–92.

17. Amy Sonnie and James Tracy, *Hillbilly Nationalists, Urban Race Rebels, and*

Black Power: Community Organizing in Radical Times (Brooklyn: Melville House, 2011), 46–48, 65, 69, 73–74, 80–83 (quote on p. 74).

18. Quoted in Sonnie and Tracy, *Hillbilly Nationalists*, 66.

19. Quoted in Sonnie and Tracy, 80.

20. Quoted in João H. Costa Vargas, *Catching Hell in the City of Angels: Life and Meanings of Blackness in South Central Los Angeles* (Minneapolis: University of Minnesota Press, 2006), 187.

21. Vargas, 110, 119, 187–90; and Hayden, *Street Wars*, 188–90. The organizing manual of the Coalition Against Police Abuse (CAPA) was modeled on BPP principles, its office was decorated with "Free Geronimo" posters, and its logo was a panther encircled by the slogan "All Power to the People." At the same time, CAPA was critical of the BPP's ideological rigidity, vanguardism, gender dynamics, and leadership style. Vargas, *Catching Hell*, 111, 118, 130–33.

22. Vargas, 188.

23. Hayden, *Street Wars*, 212.

24. Hayden, 192.

25. Hayden, 63–64, 174, 193, 231–33; and photograph by Michael Zinzun, accompanying Mike Davis, "L.A.: The Fire This Time," *CovertAction Information Bulletin*, no. 41 (Summer 1992): 17.

26. Quoted in Hayden, *Street Wars*, 33. Again, paranoia was surely a factor in this assessment. In one analysis of the riots, William Mendel of the Foreign Military Studies Office at Fort Leavenworth warned that the Bloods and Crips had conspired "to establish a truce so that they could devote their efforts towards killing Los Angeles police." (No police were killed in the uprising.) Quoted in Hayden, *Street Wars*, 230.

27. Connie Rice, *Power Concedes Nothing: One Woman's Quest for Social Justice in America, from the Courtroom to the Kill Zones* (New York: Scribner, 2012), 279.

28. Martín Sánchez-Jankowski, *Islands in the Street: Gangs and American Urban Society* (Berkeley: University of California Press, 1991), 93–200. Sánchez-Jankowski begins his chapter "The Gang and the Community" with a quote from Mao: "The people are like water and the army is like fish." Sánchez-Jankowski, *Islands in the Street*, 178.

29. Sánchez-Jankowski, 183.

30. Sánchez-Jankowski, 183–92.

31. Sánchez-Jankowski, 201.

32. Sánchez-Jankowski, 202–3.

33. Davis, *City of Quartz*, 270–74; Hayden, *Street Wars*, 87; and Sánchez-Jankowski, *Islands in the Street*, 205–6.

34. Albert DiChiara and Russell Chabot, "Gangs and the Contemporary Urban Struggle: An Unappreciated Aspect of Gangs," chap. 5 in *Gangs and Society: Alternative Perspectives*, eds. Louis Kontos, David Brotherton, Luis Barrios (New York: Columbia University Press, 2003), 82–92.

35. DiChiara and Chabot are not optimistic: "It is premature to say that gangs can become social movements of dispossessed individuals—or some other form of incipient political organization. It is clear, however, that some gang members may indeed see the gang as just that." DiChiara and Chabot, "Gangs and the Contemporary Urban Struggle," 92.

36. For a timeline of events, see David C. Brotherton and Luis Barrios, *The Almighty Latin King and Queen Nation: Street Politics and the Transformation of a New York City Gang* (New York: Columbia University Press, 2004), xvi–xix. The change in leadership was by no means the only factor in this transformation. Among others, Brotherton and Barrios list "the involvement of radical intellectuals," the ALKQN's origins as a prison gang (that "avoid[s] parochial turf wars"), "the political development of and demands of the female members," "anticolonial consciousness," and "the absence of any radical, alternative, political and social movement for the Latino/a working class." Brotherton and Barrios, 25.

37. Brotherton and Barrios, 269.

38. Brotherton and Barrios, 25.

39. These changes are outlined in two tables: table 1.4, "A Comparison of Street Organizations and Gangs," and table 8.3, "Comparative Organizational Characteristics of the ALKQN before and after Reform," in Brotherton and Barrios, 24 and 209, respectively.

40. Brotherton and Barrios, 289.

41. Brotherton and Barrios, 157.

42. They continue: "The worst example of this post-reform revanchism was the anti-political gangsterism of a group that called itself 'Gangster Killer Kings,' which worked mostly in the Brooklyn area. Its leader, King J., had formerly been a devout supporter of reform, but with the heightened attention of law enforcement and the successful conviction of their leader, he had become disillusioned and seemed to have given up on most of his own ideals about community uplift and pan-Latino resistance: 'I've had enough of this political shit. . . . It's the politics that's got us into this shit in the first place.'" Brotherton and Barrios, 271–72.

43. Brotherton and Barrios, 333.

44. Quoted in Hayden, *Street Wars*, 107.

45. Will Cooley, "'Stones Run It': Taking Back Control of Organized Crime in Chicago, 1940–1975," *Journal of Urban History* 37, no. 6 (2001): 913–14, 918.

46. Quoted in Cooley, "'Stones Run It'," 919. The Stones did make efforts to keep what they considered the worst drugs out of the Black neighborhoods. In the 1960s, the Rangers enforced a ban on heroin until key leaders were imprisoned and the Italian mob took over the drug market. Then, in the 1980s, the El Rukns refused to tolerate the sale of crack cocaine. But, again, after their leadership was imprisoned, the vacuum was filled by the Irish and

Italian mobs, who pushed the drug. Natalie Y. Moore and Lance Williams, *The Almighty Black P Stone Nation: The Rise, Fall, and Resurgence of an American Gang* (Chicago: Lawrence Hill Books, 2011), 249.

47. Bloom and Martin, *Black against Empire*, 227.

48. Bloom and Martin, 227.

49. Moore and Williams, *Almighty Black P Stone Nation*, 35, 38.

50. Moore and Williams, 5.

51. Cooley, "Stones Run It," 916–17.

52. Moore and Williams, *Almighty Black P Stone Nation*, 24–25.

53. J. Sakai, "Blackstone Rangers: U.S. Experiment Using 'Gangs' to Repress Black Community Rebellion (1976)," in *The "Dangerous Class" and Revolutionary Theory: Thoughts on the Making of the Lumpen/Proletariat* (Montreal: Kersplebedeb, 2017), 283–84.

54. No Disciples were prosecuted—perhaps because the Disciples were not viewed as a political threat. Moore and Williams, *Almighty Black P Stone Nation*, 128.

55. Moore and Williams, *Almighty Black P Stone Nation*, 132.

56. Moore and Williams, 152–53, 192; and Sakai, "Blackstone Rangers," 299.

57. Moore and Williams, *Almighty Black P Stone Nation*, 201.

58. Moore and Williams, 40–41.

59. Moore and Williams, 113.

60. Moore and Williams, 82.

61. Sakai, "Blackstone Rangers," 288; Moore and Williams, *Almighty Black P Stone Nation*, 116–122; and, Cooley, "'Stones Run It'," 911, 915–22.

62. That this was the purpose of the federal funding is indicated by the Woodlawn Organization's application to the Office of Economic Opportunity: "The Ranger leadership met and decided not to participate in the riots but, more importantly, decided to make an organized effort to prevent similar violence in Woodlawn. The following plan was developed and carried out by the Rangers in conjunction with the Chicago Police Department, the Woodlawn Organization, and the First Presbyterian Church. First, the Ranger leadership manned a twenty-four hour phone service at the Church. . . . The Ranger leadership, in response to calls, went to the site of possible disturbances and dispersed the youth involved. . . . Secondly, Ranger members were instructed to call if approached by anyone inciting them to riot. There was one such incident in which the person inciting to riot was identified and his name turned over to the Police. . . . The Rangers' action was one of the most relevant reasons that the on-going riots were prevented from taking place in Woodlawn." Quoted in Sakai, "Blackstone Rangers," 282–83.

63. Quoted in Moore and Williams, *Almighty Black P Stone Nation*, 60.

64. Quoted in Moore and Williams, 82.

65. Quoted in Sakai, "Blackstone Rangers," 285. Sakai interprets the strategy as

"a disguised Vietnam-style counterinsurgency program." Sakai, "Blackstone Rangers," 284. Recalling very different experiences from the same period, Tom Hayden notes his own reservations about the OEO. In the late sixties, Hayden was organizing with the Newark Community Union Project. The OEO opened offices in exactly the neighborhoods where the NCUP was active. While the NCUP was trying to develop grassroots leadership and alter power relations, the OEO's antipoverty program served to maintain the social hierarchy by "selecting, managing, and co-opting those 'respectable' leaders of the poor, while at the same time undermining any basis for independent efforts, especially by more militant or nationalist community groups." Hayden, *Street Wars*, 270–72.

66. Sakai, *The "Dangerous Class" and Revolutionary Theory*, 6.

67. Don Hamerquist, "Added Thoughts on Repression," unpublished manuscript, July 2, 2020.

68. This section is largely drawing from information in Hamerquist, "Added Thoughts on Repression." That there were multiple strategies at work, Moore and Williams agree: "Solutions differed. The police didn't engage with young people; instead they took a hostile street approach. . . . [The] government, nonprofits, and foundations began funding initiatives" to provide "jobs or education opportunities to you black males," while "the philanthropic community [began] to dispense its dollars into the [Stones'] organization." At the same time, the Reverend John Fry of the First Presbyterian Church sought to "reduce teenage violence . . . [by] helping the Stones establish relationships with other South Side institutions and introducing the Stones to political, social, and economic opportunities." Moore and Williams, *Almighty Black P Stone Nation*, 52.

About the precise nature of the Stones' relationship with the church, Moore and Williams are less certain. They note that other clergy suspected that Fry was manipulating the gang. The police openly accused him of sheltering criminals, a point at least some of the Stones conceded. Moore and Williams, *Almighty Black P Stone Nation*, 60–61, and 105.

The Reverend Fry, for his part, defended both the Church's involvement and the Stones themselves: "We have found that the Blackstone Rangers are an organization of great influence and promise. They are not a gang. They are a community organization. They organized originally in order to survive in a very hostile and violent environment. They quickly came to substantial size and prominence. They are determined to use their numerical strength, and to hold themselves together for the single purpose of maintaining hope for full justice, real equality, and freedom in fact, and in the hearts of all black brothers. . . . We shall maintain our friendship with and support of the Blackstone Rangers." Quoted in Moore and Williams, *Almighty Black P Stone Nation*, 109–10.

69. In the first years of the twenty-first century, J. Sakai wrote that "what were once youth gangs . . . now are sometimes Black paramilitary mafias . . . policing and perhaps semi-governing small territories where poor communities of New Afrikans live." J. Sakai, "The Shock of Recognition," in *Confronting Fascism: Discussion Documents for a Militant Movement* (Montreal: Kersplebedeb, 2017), 171 (see also 179–81).

70. Bloom and Martin, *Black against Empire*, 449n4.

71. Quoted in Moore and Williams, *Almighty Black P Stone Nation,* 96–97.

72. Bloom and Martin, *Black against Empire*, 235.

73. Sonnie and Tracy, *Hillbilly Nationalists*, 85.

74. Quoted in Moore and Williams, *Almighty Black P Stone Nation*, 97–98.

75. Moore and Williams, 98.

76. Stephen Shames and Bobby Seale, *Power to the People: The World of the Black Panthers* (New York: Abrams, 2016), 130.

77. Bloom and Martin, *Black against Empire*, 227–28.

78. Quoted in Bloom and Martin, 228.

79. Quoted in Bloom and Martin, 229.

80. Moore and Williams, *Almighty Black P Stone Nation*, 99. A similar plan achieved greater success in Los Angeles, where the Panthers were involved in a dispute with the culturally nationalist US organization over the leadership of the Black Student Union and the direction of the Black Studies program at UCLA. The FBI sought to make the most of this rivalry. In a November 25, 1968, memo, FBI Director J. Edgar Hoover noted that "it is taking on the aura of gang warfare with attendant threats of murder and reprisals" and expressed his intention "to fully capitalize" on the conflict and "creat[e] further dissension . . . crippling the [BPP]." One field office replied: "The Los Angeles Office is currently preparing an anonymous letter for Bureau approval which will be sent to the Los Angeles Black Panther Party supposedly from a member of the 'US' organization in which it will be stated that the youth group of the 'US' organization . . . plans to ambush leaders of the [BPP] in Los Angeles. It is hoped this counter-intelligence measure will result in an 'US' and [Panther] vendetta." The conflict finally came to a head on January 17, 1969, when US members killed Bunchy Carter, along with another Slauson-turned-Panther, Jon Huggins, as they left a Black Student Union meeting. Bloom and Martin, *Black against Empire*, 218–19.

   While the FBI's role here was certainly disgraceful, historians Floyd Hayes and Judson Jeffries argue: "The Panthers and Us made it somewhat easy for the government to play them against each other. After all, the elements for an explosion were potentially already in place." Hayes and Jeffries speculate that the tension between the organizations may have been, at least in part, a legacy of the gang backgrounds of many of their members: "During the mid- to late 1960s, two of the most notorious gangs in Los Angeles were the Gladiators and the Slausons. According to former Panthers and Us members, these street gangs were fertile recruiting ground for both groups. For the most part, Us recruited from the Gladiators, whereas some of the Slausons joined the Los Angeles Black Panthers. . . . Because the Slausons and Gladiators were rival gangs, it is not farfetched to believe that some of the former gang members may have continued to harbor ill will toward one another." Floyd W. Hayes III and Judson L. Jeffries, "*Us* Does Not Stand for United Slaves!," in *Black Power in the Belly of the Beast*, ed. Judson L. Jeffries (Urbana: University of Illinois Press, 2006), 81.

81. Ward Churchill and Jim Vander Wall, *The COINTELPRO Papers: Documents from the FBI's Secret Wars against Domestic Dissent* (Boston: South End Press, 1990), 139–40.

82. Moore and Williams, *Almighty Black P Stone Nation*, 98.

83. Quoted in Moore and Williams, 5.

84. Sakai, "Blackstone Rangers," 281.

85. Sakai, 289, 288.

86. Sakai, 288.

87. Tilly refers to "war making and state making" as "quintessential protection rackets" and "our largest examples of organized crime." Charles Tilly, "War Making and State Making as Organized Crime," in *Bringing the State Back In*, eds. Peter B. Evans, Dietrich Reuschemeyer, and Theda Skocpol (Cambridge: Cambridge University Press, 1994), 169.

88. Tilly, "War Making and State Making," 170, 173.

89. Tilly argues that the support of other authorities is more important than that of the populace. Tilly, 171.

90. Tilly's account is broadly in line with Weber's: "The development of the modern state is set in motion everywhere by a decision of the prince to dispossess the independent, 'private' bearers of administrative power who exist alongside him, that is all those in personal possession of the means of administration and the conduct of war, the organisation of finance and politically deployable goods of all kinds. The whole process is a complete parallel to the development of the capitalist enterprise (*Betrieb*) through the gradual expropriation of independent producers." Max Weber, "The Profession and Vocation of Politics," in *Political Writings*, eds. Peter Lassman and Ronald Speirs (Cambridge: Cambridge University Press, 2005), 316.

In Hobbesian terms, this account recalls the "*Common-wealth by Acquisition*," in which "the Sovereign Power is acquired by Force," rather than "Soveraignty by Institution," in which "Soveraign Power is conferred by the consent of the People assembled." Hobbes admits—in fact he insists—that functionally the two types of government "differeth . . . onely in this, That men who choose their Soveraign, do it for fear of one another, and not of him whom they Institute," while those who are conquered "subject them-selves, to him they are afraid of." Thomas Hobbes, *Leviathan, or the Matter, Forme and Power of a Commonwealth, Ecclesiastiall and Civill*, ed. A. R. Waller (Cambridge: Cambridge University Press, 1935), 120, 139.

As Tilly's account clarifies, even this difference is largely illusory, the process of institution being merely a method for justifying and stabiliz-ing what has already been established by force. In this version, the social contract is itself an instrument of war. The civil war does not end with the sovereign's peace but continues through "other means." Legitimacy is a weapon in that struggle, and counterinsurgency theory suggests that as such it may be decisive. See, for instance, U.S. Army, *Counterinsurgency*, Field Manual 3-24 (Washington, DC: Dept. of the Army, 2006), 1-113.

91. Stergios Skaperdas and Constantinos Syropoulos, "Gangs as Primitive States," in *The Economics of Organised Crime*, eds. Gianluca Fiorentini and Sam Peltzman (Cambridge: Cambridge University Press, 1997), 62. Recent research examining thirty criminal organizations in Medellín, Colombia, concludes that "states operate in an uneasy duopoly of coercion, rule, and taxation with urban gangs." Under this model, the government and the gang represent "two firms selling differentiated but substitutable services." Intriguingly, the researchers note that for most gangs the income from ex-tortion is "modest," and a "more important motive for governing" rests in the hope that "providing order wins the loyalty of the residents," which in turn "helps protect the gang's physical security and illicit income from com-petitors and . . . police." Christopher Blattman, et al., "Gang Rule: Under-standing and Countering Criminal Governance," pre-publication, SocArXiv Papers, https://osf.io/preprints/socarxiv/5nyqs, accessed February 5, 2021), 40, 3, 17-18.

92. Skaperdas and Syropoulos, "Gangs as Primitive States," 74. In his comment on their paper, published in the same collection, William J. Baumol fol-lows this argument through to its logical conclusion, unknowingly echoing Tilly: "A little study of history, much of it unfortunately contemporary, sug-gests . . . that there is also much to be learned from a reversal of the com-parison, this time not thinking of gangs as quasi-governments, but rather by interpreting most governments in human history as gangster associations." William J. Baumol, "Discussion," in *The Economics of Organised Crime*, eds. Gianluca Fiorentini and Sam Peltzman (Cambridge: Cambridge University Press, 1997), 83.

93. Tilly, "War Making and State Making as Organized Crime," 170, 185-86. On the specific ways the need for legitimacy constrains counterinsurgency operations, see U.S. Army, *Counterinsurgency*, especially 1-149 ("Sometimes, the More You Protect Your Force the Less Secure You May Be"), 1-150 ("Sometimes, the More Force is Used, the Less Effective It Is"), 1-151 ("The

More Successful the Counterinsurgency Is, the Less Force Can Be Used and the More Risk Must Be Accepted"), and 1-152 ("Sometimes Doing Nothing Is the Best Reaction").

94. U.S. Army, 1-115.

95. U.S. Army, 1-113.

96. "Political Factors Are Primary." U.S. Army, *Counterinsurgency*, 1-123.

97. Bloom and Martin, *Black against Empire*, 186–87.

98. Hayden, *Street* Wars, 308; Omari L. Dyson, Kevin L. Brooks, and Judson L. Jeffries, "'Brotherly Love Can Kill You': The Philadelphia Branch of the Black Panther Party," in *Comrades: A Local History of the Black Panther Party*, ed. Judson L. Jeffries (Bloomington: Indiana University Press, 2007), 228–30; and Jeffries and Foley, "To Live and Die in L.A.," 269.

99. Alonso, "Racialized Identities and the Formation of Black Gangs," 669–71; and Hayden, *Street Wars*, 167, 308.

100. Davis, *City of Quartz*, 298–99.

101. U.S. Army, *Counterinsurgency*, 1-58. Emphasis added.

102. Bloom and Martin, *Black against Empire*, 381–82.

103. Umoja, "The Black Liberation Army and the Radical Legacy," 234.

104. Quoted in Stanley Nelson, dir., *The Black Panthers: Vanguard of the Revolution* (Firelight Films, 2015).

105. Elaine Brown, *A Taste of Power: A Black Woman's Story* (New York: Random House, 1994), 333.

106. Quoted in Nelson, *The Black Panthers*.

107. Quoted in David Hilliard and Keith Kent Zimmerman, *Huey: Spirit of the Panther* (Philadelphia: Basic Books, 2006), 202.

108. Hilliard, 3–4.

109. Hilliard, 200.

110. Hilliard, 12, 18.

111. Hilliard, 45–46.

112. Hilliard, 200–201.

113. Elaine Brown recalled a conversation she'd had with "several of the Brothers" one night: "Chortling, they had suggested that 'if all else failed' the party had the ability to become a kind of black version of the Mafia. We had the guns and the men, they boasted." Brown, *Taste of Power*, 444.

114. Quoted in Umoja, "Black Liberation Army and the Radical Legacy," 234.

115. Quoted in Hilliard, *Huey*, 205.

116. Bloom and Martin, *Black against Empire*, 383.

117. Judson L. Jeffries, "An Unexamined Chapter of Black Panther History," in *Black Power in the Belly of the Beast* (Urbana: University of Illinois Press, 2006), 214.

118. Bloom and Martin, *Black against Empire*, 342.

119. Ollie A. Johnson III, "Explaining the Demise of the Black Panther Party:

The Role of Internal Factors," in *The Black Panther Party (Reconsidered)*, ed. Charles E. Jones (Baltimore: Black Classic Press, 2005), 398.

120. Johnson, 399–407.

121. Lorenzo Komboa Ervin, *Anarchism and the Black Revolution: The Idea of Black Autonomy* (Denver: P&L Press, n.d.), 134–46. Lorenzo Ervin was simultaneously a member of a street gang and the NAACP youth group in Chattanooga. He was drafted into the army but court-martialed for antiwar agitation. Once discharged, he joined SNCC just before it merged with the BPP. Ervin, *Anarchism and the Black Revolution*, 323.

122. Bakunin knew better. "Crime," he wrote, "[is] the privilege of the State. What is permitted to the State is forbidden to the individual. Such is the maxim of all governments. . . . Crime is the necessary condition of the very existence of the State, and it therefore constitutes its exclusive monopoly." Mikhail Bakunin, "Ethics: Morality of the State," in *Classic Writings in Anarchist Criminology: A Historical Dismantling of Punishment and Domination*, eds. Anthony J. Nocella II, Mark Seis, and Jeff Shantz (Chico, CA: AK Press, 2020), 98.

123. Gompert and Gordon, *War by Other Means*, xxxvii.

124. Christian Parenti, "Crime as Social Control," *Social Justice* 27, no. 3 (2000): 43–49.

Street Fights, Gang Wars, and Insurrections: Proud Boys versus Antifa (versus Police)

1. For a firsthand account of that day, with particular attention to the role of the Proud Boys, see Luke Mogelson, "Among the Insurrectionists," *New Yorker*, January 15, 2021, https://www.newyorker.com/magazine/2021/01/25/among-the-insurrectionists.

2. Pilar Melendez, William Bredderman, and Blake Montgomery, "'Didn't Have a Choice': Vet Was Climbing through Broken Window When She Was Shot Dead," *Daily Beast*, January 8, 2021, https://www.thedailybeast.com/one-woman-shot-six-hospitalized-as-trump-loving-mob-swarms-capitol. Of the other three deaths on January 6, two were the result of hypertensive atherosclerotic cardiovascular disease and one of an amphetamine overdose. Capitol Police officer Brian Sicknick died the following day after suffering a stroke. Rick Massimo, "Medical Examiner: Capitol Police Officer Sicknick Died of Stroke; Death Ruled 'Natural,'" WTOP News, April 19, 2021, https://wtop.com/dc/2021/04/medical-examiner-capitol-police-officer-sicknick-died-of-stroke-death-ruled-natural.

3. Jason Wilson, "How US Police Failed to Stop the Rise of the Far Right and the Capitol Attack," *Guardian*, January 17, 2021.

4. Mara Hvistendahl and Alleen Brown, "Armed Vigilantes Antagonizing Protesters Have Received a Warm Reception from Police," *The Intercept*, June 19, 2020, https://theintercept.com/2020/06/19/militia-vigilantes-police-brutality-protests; and Ryan Devereaux, "The Thin Blue Line between Violent Pro-Trump Militias and Police," *The Intercept*, August 28, 2020, https://theintercept.com/2020/08/28/kyle-rittenhouse-violent-pro-trump-militias-police.

5. Brandy Zadrozny and Ben Collins, "Antifa Rumors Spread on Local Social Media with No Evidence," NBC News, June 2, 2020, https://www.nbcnews.com/tech/tech-news/antifa-rumors-spread-local-social-media-no-evidence-n1222486; Jason Wilson, "Rightwing Vigilantes on Armed Patrol After Fake Rumours of Antifa Threat," *Guardian*, June 6, 2020, https://www.theguardian.com/us-news/2020/jun/06/rightwing-vigilante-armed-antifa-protests; Brandy Zadrozny and Ben Collins, "In Klamath Falls, Oregon, Victory Declared over Antifa, Which Never Showed Up," NBC News, June 6, 2020, https://www.nbcnews.com/tech/social-media/klamath-falls-oregon-victory-declared-over-Antifa-which-never-showed-n1226681.

6. Jason Wilson, "Armed Civilian Roadblocks in Oregon Town Fuel Fears over Vigilantism," *Guardian*, September 16, 2020; and, Jason Wilson, "Social Media Disinformation on US West Coast Blazes 'Spreading Faster Than Fire'," *Guardian*, September 14, 2020.

7. Stanislav Vysotsky, *American Antifa: The Tactics, Culture, and Practice of Militant Antifascism* (New York: Routledge, 2021), 133

8. See, for example, Leighton Akio Woodhouse, "After Charlottesville, the American Far Right Is Tearing Itself Apart," *The Intercept*, September 21, 2017, https://theintercept.com/2017/09/21/gavin-mcinnes-alt-right-proud-boys-richard-spencer-charlottesville.

9. On August 16, 2017, an NPR/PBS poll found that 5 percent of Americans "mostly agreed" with Antifa. In raw numbers, that would represent between seven and eight million people. Nigel Copsey and Samuel Merrill, *Understanding 21st-Century Militant Anti-Fascism* (Centre for Research and Evidence on Security Threats, 2021), 39.

10. Amy Goodman, "Cornel West and Rev. Traci Blackmon: Clergy in Charlottesville Were Trapped by Torch-Wielding Nazis," *Democracy Now*, August 14, 2017, https://www.democracynow.org/2017/8/14/cornel_west_rev_toni_blackmon_clergy.

11. See, for instance: Spencer Sunshine, "Has the 'Alt-Right' Met Its Gettysburg?" *Truthout*, August 26, 2017, https://truthout.org/articles/has-the-alt-right-met-its-gettysburg.

12. David Duke called the event a "turning point." Quoted in Libby Nelson, "'Why We Voted for Donald Trump': David Duke Explains the White Supremacist Charlottesville Protests," *Vox*, August 12, 2017, https://www.vox.com/2017/8/12/16138358/charlottesville-protests-david-duke-kkk.

13. Here is the full sentence: "We condemn in the strongest possible terms this egregious display of hatred, bigotry and violence on many sides." He then repeated: "On many sides." A White House spokesperson later clarified: "The President was condemning hatred, bigotry and violence from all sources and all sides. There was violence between protesters and counterprotesters today." Both quoted in Jenna Johnson and John Wagner, "Trump Condemns Charlottesville Violence but Doesn't Single Out White Nationalists," *Washington Post*, August 12, 2017.

14. Vysotsky, *American Antifa*, 76. Jason Kessler, the chief organizer of the Charlottesville rally, confided in an online chat room, "We're going to be triggering Antifa to protest and force the Alt-Light's hand." Quoted in Emily Gorcenski, "The Proud Boys: A Republican Party Street Gang," *Political Research Associates*, February 28, 2019, https://www.politicalresearch .org/2019/02/28/proud-boys.

15. Quoted in Southern Poverty Law Center, "SPLC Statement on Proud Boys Rally in Portland, Ore.," September 25, 2020, https://www.splcenter.org/ presscenter/splc-statement-proud-boys-rally-portland-ore.

16. Josef Schneider, in conversation, 2017.

17. Quoted in Anti-Defamation League, "Proud Boys," https://www.adl.org/ proudboys, accessed June 2021.

18. Southern Poverty Law Center, "Proud Boys," https://www.splcenter.org/ fighting-hate/extremist-files/group/proud-boys, accessed June 2021.

19. Quoted in Kyle Cheney, "Wray Says Russia Engaged in 'Very Active Efforts' to Interfere in Election, Damage Biden," *Politico*, September 17, 2020, https://www.politico.com/news/2020/09/17/fbi-director-russia-election -meddling-416839.

20. Vysotsky, *American Antifa*, 169.

21. "Their style was an exaggerated version of the traditional unskilled laborer." Tiffini A. Travis and Perry Hardy, *Skinheads: A Guide to an American Subculture* (Santa Barbara: Greenwood, 2012), xiii.

22. Timothy S. Brown, "Subcultures, Pop Music and Politics: Skinheads and 'Nazi Rock' in England and Germany," in *White Riot: Punk Rock and the Politics of Race*, eds. Stephen Duncombe and Maxwell Tremblay (New York: Verso, 2011), 121; and Todd Ferguson, "'Taking It Back, Making It Strong!': The Boundary Establishment and Maintenance Practices of a Montréal Anti-Racist Skinhead Gang" (master's thesis, McGill University, 2002), 3–6.

   Typical of fascists, racist skins mythologize their past, insisting that the culture originated with pro-Nazi British youth in the 1930s. However, as one scholar writes, "With little or no evidence to support their own claims, the racist skinhead theory of the subculture emerging from racist white youth in Britain or elsewhere can be disregarded with a high degree of confidence." Ferguson, "'Taking It Back, Making It Strong!,'" 4.

23. Brown, "Subcultures, Pop Music and Politics," 122, 127; and Vysotsky, *American Antifa*, 113.

24. As Eric Anderson summed up in his study of one racist crew, "As skinheads, . . . the S.F. Skins were able to use the medium of violence as a means of expressing their self-esteem, collective group image, and significance, within a new and seemingly more appropriate subculture context." Eric Anderson, "Skinheads: From San Francisco Hardcore Punks to Skinheads," in Tiffini A. Travis and Perry Hardy, *Skinheads: A Guide to an American Subculture* (Santa Barbara: Greenwood, 2012), 142.

25. Stephen Duncombe and Maxwell Tremblay, "White Power," in *White Riot: Punk Rock and the Politics of Race* (London: Verso, 2011), 115.

26. Brown, "Subcultures, Pop Music and Politics," 127; and Vysotsky, *American Antifa*, 47.

27. John Clarke, "The Skinheads and the Magical Recovery of Community," in *White Riot: Punk Rock and the Politics of Race*, eds. Stephen Duncombe and Maxwell Tremblay (New York: Verso, 2011), 116. Emphasis in original.

28. Quoted in Clarke, "The Skinheads and the Magical Recovery of Community," 118. Punctuation edited.

29. Probably the first racist skinhead gang in the United States was Romantic Violence, founded in Chicago in 1984, but soon there were others all around the country: Death Squad Skins and Gestapo Skins (both in the Bay Area), Skinhead Army (Milwaukee), Confederate Hammerskins (Dallas and then elsewhere), the American Firm (Orange County), the Bootboys and Bomber Boys (both from San Diego). Travis and Hardy, *Skinheads*, xxi, 62–64, 86; and Elinor Langer, *A Hundred Little Hitlers: The Death of a Black Man, the Trial of a White Racist, and the Rise of the Neo-Nazi Movement in America* (New York: Picador, 2003), 186, 196.

30. Shane Burley, *Fascism Today: What It Is and How to End It* (Chico, CA: AK Press, 2017), 123. "Skinheads are our front-line warriors," WAR organizers bragged. Quoted in Langer, *A Hundred Little Hitlers*, 181.

31. Langer, 187.

32. Burley, *Fascism Today*, 162.

33. Langer, *A Hundred Little Hitlers*, 12–13, 53, 200.

34. Anna Stitt, "Fighting Back: The Rise of Anti-Racist Action in Minneapolis," *Minneculture In-Depth*, KFAI, [2020], https://www.kfai.org/minneculture-in-depth-fighting-back-the-rise-of-anti-racist-action-in-minneapolis.

35. "The Baldies were a multi-racial group of skinheads in Minneapolis who for the most part were apolitical until the nazi skinheads came on the scene, which immediately politicized them." Martin Sprouse and Tim Yohannan, "Kieran Knutson of Anti-Racist Action, Interview in *Maximumrocknroll*," in *White Riot: Punk Rock and the Politics of Race*, eds. Stephen Duncombe and Maxwell Tremblay (New York: Verso, 2011), 147.

‎

‎

‎

‎

‎

‎

‎

‎

‎

‎

‎

‎

‎

‎

‎

‎

‎

‎
‎
‎
‎
‎

36. "Episode Four: The Minneapolis Baldies and Anti Racist Action," *It Did Happen Here*, podcast transcript, http://itdidhappenherepodcast.com/transcripts/episode4_transcript.html.

37. Mark Bray, *Antifa: The Anti-Fascist Handbook* (Brooklyn: Melville House, 2017), 66; and "Fighting Back: The Rise of Anti-Racist Action in Minneapolis."

38. Quoted in Southern Poverty Law Center, "Roots of ARA," *Intelligence Report*, May 16, 2013, https://www.splcenter.org/fighting-hate/intelligence-report/2013/roots-ara.

39. Quoted in Sprouse and Yohannan, "Kieran Knutson of Anti-Racist Action," 149.

40. "Fighting Back: The Rise of Anti-Racist Action in Minneapolis."

41. Quoted in Bray, *Antifa*, 167. Ellipses in original. Mic Crenshaw recounts these conversations:

    "Hey man, are you guys white power?" . . .

    "Yeah, man, we're the White Knights." . . .

    "Well, you know, that's not gonna fly around here. We're going to give you a chance to denounce that shit, and the next time we see you, if you're still claiming white power then there's . . . going to be a problem." "Episode Four: The Minneapolis Baldies."

42. Quoted in "Fighting Back: The Rise of Anti-Racist Action in Minneapolis."

43. "Fighting Back: The Rise of Anti-Racist Action in Minneapolis." The police used the same approach, isolating white members of the Baldies and pressuring them to leave the group. "Fighting Back: The Rise of Anti-Racist Action in Minneapolis."

44. Bray, *Antifa*, 167–68. The Baldies' approach to confrontation carried over to Portland. One activist from the period later recalled: "The rule that we tried to put forth was, do not attack people while they're alone. And the reason for this was that we believed that individual Nazis, boneheads, whatever, could be converted, and some of them were." Quoted in Vysotsky, *American Antifa*, 94–95.

45. Quoted in Rory McGowan, "Claim No Easy Victories: An Analysis of Anti-Racist Action and Its Contributions to the Building of a Radical Anti-Racist Movement," *Northeastern Anarchist*, September 30, 2021, https://theanarchistlibrary.org/library/rory-mcgowan-claim-no-easy-victories.

46. Quoted in Sprouse and Yohannan, "Kieran Knutson of Anti-Racist Action," 147.

47. "Fighting Back: The Rise of Anti-Racist Action in Minneapolis."

48. "Episode Four: The Minneapolis Baldies and Anti Racist Action." "It's important to talk to people in the scene about racism and not letting it be acceptable," Knutson later told interviewers. "If you are going out there and fighting and the scene isn't going to be behind you, then it's not very

effective. . . . One of the reasons why the Baldies won so much isn't because we're on some macho trip or that we're all huge people, but because we've been able to get the numbers to support us and that's what's most import-ant." Quoted in Sprouse and Yohannan, "Kieran Knutson of Anti-Racist Action," 149.

49. "Episode Four: The Minneapolis Baldies and Anti Racist Action"; and Tra-vis and Hardy, *Skinheads*, 65.

50. Bray, *Antifa*, 69.

51. Quoted in "How the Midwest Was Won: The Bloody Rise of Anti-Rac-ist Action," It's Going Down, February 16, 2018, https://itsgoingdown.org/ midwest-won-bloody-rise-ara.

52. Quoted in "How the Midwest Was Won."

53. "Episode Four: The Minneapolis Baldies and Anti Racist Action."

54. "Episode Four: The Minneapolis Baldies and Anti Racist Action"; "Fighting Back: The Rise of Anti-Racist Action in Minneapolis"; Travis and Hardy, *Skinheads*, 65; and Sprouse and Yohannan, "Kieran Knutson of Anti-Racist Action," 148.

55. "Episode Four: The Minneapolis Baldies and Anti Racist Action."

56. Bray, *Antifa*, 57, 67. For a short history of Anti-Fascist Action, see Copsey and Merrill, *Understanding 21st-Century Militant Anti-Fascism*, 52.

57. Bray, *Antifa*, 67; "Fighting Back: The Rise of Anti-Racist Action in Minne-apolis"; Sprouse and Yohannan, "Kieran Knutson of Anti-Racist Action," 147; and Copsey and Merrill, *Understanding 21st-Century Militant Anti-Fascism*, 13–14.

58. Kate Sharpley Library, Class War, and Three Way Fight, "Anti-Fascism Now," in *Beating Fascism: Anarchist Anti-Fascism in Theory and Practice*, ed. Anna Key (London: Kate Sharpley Library, 2006), 45–46; "Fighting Back: The Rise of Anti-Racist Action in Minneapolis"; and McGowan, "Claim No Easy Victories."

59. Quoted in Travis and Hardy, *Skinheads*, 66.

60. "How the Midwest Was Won"; "Militant Tactics in Anti-Fascist Orga-nizing: Interview Transcript," interview with Kieran [Knutson] for KPFA Radio's *Against the Grain* by the programs co-producer Sasha Lilley, *Three Way Fight*, April 26, 2017, http://threewayfight.blogspot.com/2017/04/militant -tactics-in-anti-fascist.html.

61. Lola, "On the Prowl: Notes on Anti-Racist Action and Developing Anti-Fascist Strategies in Toronto," in *Beating Fascism: Anarchist Anti-Fascism in Theory and Practice*, ed. Anna Key (London: Kate Sharpley Library, 2006), 34.

Rock Against Racism (RAR) was another borrowing from the United Kingdom. In August 1976, a small group of activists associated with the Socialist Workers Party formed RAR, organizing a series of concerts bringing together "Reggae, Soul, Rock'n'roll, Jazz, Funk, and Punk." Paul Gilroy, "Two Sides of Anti-Racism," in *White Riot: Punk Rock and the Politics of Race*, eds. Stephen Duncombe and Maxwell Tremblay (New York: Verso, 2011), 181–82. In its first year, Rock Against Racism organized two hundred gigs throughout the UK, mixing genres on the same stage in order to draw diverse crowds. They deliberately recruited bands that skinheads liked—notably Sham 69—so that they might attract nazis and change their thinking, sometimes through direct argument and sometimes by cultural osmosis. "If RAR meant anything," David Widgery, one of its founding members, later said, "it meant preaching to the unconverted." David Widgery, *Beating Time* (London: Chatto & Windus, 1986), 71, 80 (quotation), 104. See also, Rubika Shah, dir., *White Riot* (Film Movement: 2020).

62. Lili the Skinbird, "Associating with Racists: A Way to Promote Anti-Racism?" in *White Riot: Punk Rock and the Politics of Race*, eds. Stephen Duncombe and Maxwell Tremblay (New York: Verso, 2011), 153.

63. Southern Poverty Law Center, "Roots of ARA."

64. Kieran Knutson explained, using the language of counterinsurgency: "Militant tactics is part of our strategy, but it's not the only part. A big part of it is a battle for the hearts and minds that the fascists are trying to recruit for their base." In "Militant Tactics in Anti-Fascist Organizing."

65. Quoted in "How the Midwest Was Won."

66. This possibility was first mentioned to me by Effie Baum in conversation, 2019.

67. "Movement organizations can offer people few selective incentives to participate. Instead, they try to exploit people's preexisting ties—to friends, say, or to the church—in recruiting them, and then rely on the solidarity created within the movement and organization to sustain their participation." Francesca Polletta, *Freedom Is an Endless Meeting: Democracy in American Social Movements* (Chicago: University of Chicago Press, 2002), 210.

68. Quoted in Wes Enzinna, "This Is War and We Intend to Win," *Mother Jones*, May/June 2017, https://www.motherjones.com/politics/2017/04/anti -racist-antifa-tinley-park-five.

69. McGowan, "Claim No Easy Victories."

70. Quoted in "How the Midwest Was Won."

71. Quoted in Sprouse and Yohannan, "Kieran Knutson of Anti-Racist Action," 148.

72. Quoted in "How the Midwest Was Won."

73. Burley, *Fascism Today*, 199.

74. "Fighting Back: The Rise of Anti-Racist Action in Minneapolis"; and "How the Midwest Was Won."

75. Quoted in "How the Midwest Was Won."

76. "Episode Five: They Thought We Were Everywhere: The Portland ARA,"

It Did Happen Here, podcast transcript, http://itdidhappenherepodcast.com/transcripts/episode5_transcript.html.

77. In March 1986, four skinheads, including members of POWAR (Preservation of the White American Race) stabbed and killed a white man during a robbery outside the club Satyricon. Langer, *A Hundred Little Hitlers*, 11, 51, 66. In September 1988, several members of East Side White Pride, including Kyle Brewster and Ken Mieske, started a fight with a Black security guard at the downtown Safeway, leaving him stabbed and bleeding, with a punctured lung. (He survived.) Langer, *A Hundred Little Hitlers*, 95.

78. M. Treloar, "Portland History in Review: *A Hundred Little Hitlers*," Anarchist Library, "from the winter/spring 2004 issue of 'Little Beirut,'" https://theanarchistlibrary.org/library/m-treloar-portland-history-in-review-a-hundred-little-hitlers. A letter to *Willamette Week* captured the atmosphere in the punk scene, repeatedly invoking the "gang" as the model of skinhead behavior: "In the dancing 'pit' at 'hardcore' shows, male skins gang up on individuals who 'look at them funny.' . . . Female skins beat up girls in the bathroom of Pine Street Theatre, with no provocation whatever. The skinheads drink outside the venues. . . . They carry baseball bats with swastikas on them, knives, brass knuckles, etc. . . . For those of us who work at establishments frequented by skinheads, the intimidation factor inherent in gang-type activity is all too real. How can a club owner or employee ever criticize one skinhead without the fear of having all the establishment's windows broken by the gang? You can't throw out one violent skinhead without incurring the wrath and retribution of all the skinheads. The escalation of the number of skinheads in Portland in the last two years is absolutely staggering. Perhaps not very many of them are organized in groups like POWAR, but . . . it seems likely that at least some of them will be joining their lookalikes in gang-type intimidation in the future." Quoted in Langer, *A Hundred Little Hitlers*, 50.

79. Treloar, "Portland History in Review," 5.

80. "Episode Five: They Thought We Were Everywhere."

81. For a detailed account, see "Episode Seven: A Research Capacity: The Work of the CHD," *It Did Happen Here*, podcast transcript, http://itdidhappenherepodcast.com/transcripts/episode7_transcript.html. Quote is also from that source.

82. Treloar, "Portland History in Review," 5.

83. Bray, *Antifa*, 71.

84. "Fighting Back: The Rise of Anti-Racist Action in Minneapolis."

85. Kate Sharpley Library, Class War, and Three Way Fight, "Anti-Fascism Now," 46. Naturally, then, some activists came to antifascist work by first joining ARA-organized copwatch patrols. Vysotsky, *American Antifa*, 57.

86. Bray, *Antifa*, 68; and "How the Midwest Was Won."

87. Donovan, "ARA Responds to 'Fighting Words' (extracts)," in *Beating Fascism: Anarchist Anti-Fascism in Theory and Practice*, ed. Anna Key (London: Kate Sharpley Library, 2006), 39.

88. Sprouse and Yohannan, "Kieran Knutson of Anti-Racist Action," 148.

89. "Episode Five: They Thought We Were Everywhere."

90. "How the Midwest Was Won."

91. The size of individual chapters varied greatly. Detroit ARA had a "hard core of maybe eight or nine people" and "maybe a circle of forty people." "How the Midwest Was Won." At its height, Minneapolis would draw fifty people to meetings. "Fighting Back: The Rise of Anti-Racist Action in Minneapolis." In Toronto, organizing meetings would include as many as one hundred people. McGowan, "Claim No Easy Victories."

92. Quoted in Burley, *Fascism Today*, 198–99. For an elaboration of these principles and what they meant to the group's members, see "How the Midwest Was Won," *It's Going Down*.

93. Pan, in "Bonus Episode: More Fighters," *It Did Happen Here*, podcast transcript, http://itdidhappenherepodcast.com/transcripts/bonus_8_transcript.html.

94. Pan: "We used to make fun of the peckerwoods because they were just the foot soldiers of the right and we kind of became the foot soldiers of the left." "Bonus Episode: More Fighters."

95. Michael Clark, a SHARP from the time, explains this in terms that are more sophisticated and self-aware than most leftists would expect: "One of the things for me personally, that kept me from getting more involved[,] was too many rules. It's what people would nowadays call 'very woke,' right? You couldn't call a girl the B word. You had to be okay with everyone being gay, you had to be okay with everything, which, which I don't have any issue with. But it was like, I'm an old timer and I'm kind of slow, so like, I can't get woke all at once. And how woke can you be over the course of 6 months? So maybe I'll say it was morally intimidating." "Bonus Episode: More Fighters."

96. "Episode Eight: SHARPer Times," *It Did Happen Here*, podcast transcript, http://itdidhappenherepodcast.com/transcripts/episode8_transcript.html.

97. Xtn, correspondence with author, August 15, 2021.

98. McGowan, "Claim No Easy Victories."

99. One sociological source went so far as to describe them as "non-racist but fascist skinheads." Simon J. Bronner and Cindy Dell Clark, eds., *Youth Cultures in America* (Santa Barbara: Greenwood, 2016), 622.

100. Eric Pooley, "With Extreme Prejudice: A Murder in Queens Exposes the Frightening Rise of Gay-Bashing," *New York*, April 8, 1996, 37–38. Rivera's murder provides a disturbing counterpoint to the murder of Mulugeta Seraw, and it likewise prompted an upsurge in activism. As the killers went

to trial, "Gay activists led marches and protests in Rivera's name—including the first-ever gay-rights march in Queens. They held press conferences and meetings with police and city officials, heckled the mayor, and tried to get New Yorkers to wake up to the escalating street war against homosexuals. A group called the Pink Panthers launched street patrols, trying to deter the attacks, and *OutWeek* magazine began discussing the pros and cons of packing guns and shooting the bashers." Pooley, "With Extreme Prejudice," 38.

101. Travis and Hardy, *Skinheads*, 68.

102. "Episode Eight: SHARPer Times."

103. In 1990, the Coalition for Human Dignity issued a report documenting persistent police harassment of antiracist activists, including the use of the "gang" label to criminalize their organizations. Coalition for Human Dignity, "Report of the Community Defense Project on Organized Neo-Fascists in Portland, Oregon," May 18, 1990. For details from the police perspective, see Loren Christensen, *Skinhead Street Gangs* (Boulder, CO: Paladin Press, 1994), 56–63.

104. Vysotsky, *American Antifa*, 8. As one original member of SHARP put it in the early teens, "As it is today SHARP is unorganized. It lacks any central body, and for the most part anyone is free to slap a SHARP patch on their jacket and say they are a member of SHARP, when the truth is that there is no actual organization to be a member of." Travis and Hardy, *Skinheads*, 67.

105. Christensen, *Skinhead Street Gangs*, 57.

106. "Bonus Episode: More Fighters."

107. "Episode Nine: The Story of Jon Bair," *It Did Happen Here*, podcast transcript, http://itdidhappenherepodcast.com/transcripts/episode9_transcript.html.

108. "Bonus Episode: More Fighters."

109. "Episode Nine: The Story of Jon Bair."

110. "Bonus Episode: More Fighters."

111. "Episode Nine: The Story of Jon Bair."

112. "Bonus Episode: More Fighters."

113. "Fighting Back: The Rise of Anti-Racist Action in Minneapolis."

114. Quoted in "How the Midwest Was Won."

115. Xtn, preface to *Confronting Fascism: Discussion Documents for a Militant Movement* (Montreal: Kersplebedeb, 2017), 4.

116. McGowan, "Claim No Easy Victories"; and, Xtn, correspondence with author, August 15, 2021. With his permission, I'll just note that Xtn and Rory McGowan are the same person.

117. "Fighting Back: The Rise of Anti-Racist Action in Minneapolis."

118. "Fighting Back: The Rise of Anti-Racist Action in Minneapolis."

119. McGowan, "Claim No Easy Victories."

120. Vysotsky, *American Antifa*, 9. One member of Rose City Antifa told a

researcher: "We wanted to broaden the scope beyond ARA . . . beyond just racism. . . . [T]his was sort of when Antifa was becoming more of a label in Europe. . . . [We] felt part of more of an internationalist movement." Quoted in Copsey and Merrill, *Understanding 21st-Century Militant Anti-Fascism*, 18. On Northeastern Antifa's relationship with ARA: Xtn, correspondence with author, August 15, 2021.

121. "History," *Torch Network*, https://torchantifa.org/history, accessed June 2021.

122. Spencer Sunshine, correspondence with author, July 18, 2021.

123. To cite just one embarrassing example, on August 22, 2021, on the sidelines of a demonstration against the Proud Boys, one crew from the black bloc attacked a freelance journalist, knocking her to the ground, spraying her with pepper spray, and calling her a dog and a "slut." Tess Riski, "A Portland Photojournalist Describes Being Attacked by an Anonymous Leftist Protester in the Street," *Willamette Week*, September 1, 2021.

124. Xtn, correspondence with author, August 15, 2021.

125. Vysotsky, *American Antifa*, 9.

126. "Chapters," *Torch Network*, https://torchantifa.org/chapters, accessed June 2021.

127. Spencer Sunshine, correspondence with author, July 18, 2021.

128. "While antifa is, in reality, a small and loosely organized antifascist collective that utilizes militant tactics to counter the influence of far-right activists in their communities, the Proud Boys have turned them into a boogeyman that represents the whole of leftist politics. They denounce anyone they disagree with politically as a member of antifa, with McInnes going so far as to describe the group as a paramilitary arm of the Democratic Party. Flattening any distinctions between militant activists and mainstream Democratic politicians is a rhetorical trick aimed not only at delegitimizing all of the political left but also justifying their own violent actions against anyone they consider a political enemy." Southern Poverty Law Center, "Proud Boys."

129. Langer, *A Hundred Little Hitlers*, 248.

130. "Episode Eight: SHARPer Times."

131. Proud Boys sometimes wear shirts displaying the letters "RWDS": right-wing death squad. Southern Poverty Law Center, "SPLC Statement on Proud Boys Rally."

132. *Willamette Week* ran photos of Brewster standing in a group with Proud Boys and militiamen and reported that he had also been seen at a Proud Boys rally a few months before. Tess Riski and Aaron Mesh, "Kyle Brewster, Convicted in 1988 Killing of Mulugeta Seraw, Fought at Jan. 6 Pro-Trump Rally in Salem," *Willamette Week*, January 17, 2021. Organized racism has been a constant in Brewster's life. While serving his sentence for the Seraw murder, he helped to establish East Side White Pride as a prison gang. In 2006, he

returned to prison on a parole violation after becoming involved with Volks-front. Of his involvement in the January 6, 2021, melee outside the state capitol, he wrote, "And yep, i [*sic*] was part of a three on three fight with non white immigrants to this country and no part of me is sorry, remorseful or regretful about that." Quoted in "Kyle Brewster, Convicted in Notorious 1988 Hate Crime Killing, Seen at Pro-Trump Rallies in Salem, Portland," *Oregonian*, January 19, 2021.

133. Quoted in Shannon E. Reid and Matthew Valasik, *Alt-Right Gangs: A Hazy Shade of White* (Oakland: University of California Press, 2020), 14.

134. Gavin McInnes, "Introducing: The Proud Boys," *Taki's Magazine*, September 15, 2016, https://www.takimag.com/article/introducing_the_proud _boys_gavin_mcinnes.

135. McInnes, "Introducing: The Proud Boys." This figure is surely inflated. Three years later, they were claiming eight thousand members, though researchers estimated the true number was less than half that. Samantha Kutner, "Swiping Right: The Allure of Hyper Masculinity and Cryptofascism for Men Who Join the Proud Boys," International Centre for Counter-Terrorism-The Hague, May 2020, 2.

136. McInnes, "Introducing: The Proud Boys."

137. Quoted in Southern Poverty Law Center, "Proud Boys."

138. Southern Poverty Law Center, "Proud Boys."

139. Quoted in Alexandra Minna Stern, *Proud Boys and the White Ethnostate: How the Alt-Right Is Warping the American Imagination* (Boston: Beacon Press, 2019), 74–75.

140. Gavin McInnes, "We Are Not Alt-Right: The Founder Goes on Record," *Proud Boy Magazine*, [n.d.], https://archive.is/eDdDX, accessed June 2021.

141. Vysotsky, *American Antifa*, 81. On the alt-right's appropriation of Pepe and the "okay" sign, see ADL, "Okay Hand Gesture" and "Pepe the Frog," in *Hate on Display: Hate Symbols Database*, https://www.adl.org/hate-symbols.

142. Jason Wilson, "Who Are The Proud Boys, 'Western Chauvinists' Involved in Political Violence?," *Guardian*, July 14, 2018; Brendan O'Connor, "Trump's Useful Thugs: How the Republican Party Offered a Home to the Proud Boys," *Guardian*, January 21, 2021; and Mogelson, "Among the Insurrectionists."

143. Quoted in "Lost in the Proud," *This American Life*, September 22, 2017, https://www.thisamericanlife.org/626/transcript.

144. McInnes: "I'm a Western chauvinist. I'm all about the culture. Now, part of that is recognizing that white males seem to be the ones who made it and respecting that, but it doesn't mean you're not invited to the party." Quoted in "Lost in the Proud."

145. Kerry Harwin, "Police Investigate Assault on Livestreamer after Far-Right Proud Boys Descend on Portland," *Daily Beast*, September 26, 2020, https://

www.thedailybeast.com/police-investigate-assault-on-livestreamer-after-far-right-proud-boys-descend-on-portland.

146. Zoe Chace put this to McInnes directly: "'Our culture is better than yours. Our women need to stay home and make more babies. Our country has no more space for immigrants. We are being persecuted.' Those are your ideas. Those are ideas I see in white supremacist groups. Do you see that you guys have those same ideas?" "Yes, I do," McInnes admitted, though he is hardly enthusiastic about it. "And that's the plight of the right in many ways." Quoted in "Lost in the Proud."

147. Quoted in Mike German, *Thinking Like a Terrorist: Insights of a Former FBI Undercover Agent* (Washington, DC: Potomac Books, 2007), 16; Anti-Defamation League, "14 Words," *Hate on Display: Hate Symbols Database*, adl.org/hate-symbols, accessed November 12, 2021.

148. O'Connor, "Trump's Useful Thugs." Samantha Kutner notes that McInnes has expressly identified the words as synonymous. In his memoir, he wrote that in Taiwan "they get mad if you say White because that is politically incorrect. The term is Western." Quoted in Kutner, "Swiping Right," 15.

149. "Lost in the Proud."

150. McInnes, "Introducing: The Proud Boys."

151. Quoted in Wilson, "Who Are the Proud Boys."

152. Julia R. DeCook, "Memes and Symbolic Violence: #Proudboys and the Use of Memes for Propaganda and the Construction of Collective Identity," *Learning, Media and Technology* 43, no. 4 (2018): 500; Shane Burley, "Alt-Right Gangs: A Q&A with Shannon Reid, Co-Author of *Alt-Right Gangs: A Hazy Shade of White*," *Political Research Associates*, December 16, 2020, https://www.politicalresearch.org/2020/12/16/alt-right-gangs.

153. Quoted in Cassie Miller, "Why Are the Proud Boys So Violent? Ask Gavin McInnes," *Southern Poverty Law Center*, October 18, 2018, https://www.splcenter.org/hatewatch/2018/10/18/why-are-proud-boys-so-violent-ask-gavin-mcinnes. "An examination of hours of interviews and statements from Biggs, Nordean and other Proud Boys leaders shows that in addition to the group's often hateful and discriminatory ideology, violence has always been at the core of the group's identity." Tom Dreisbach, "Conspiracy Charges Bring Proud Boys' History of Violence into Spotlight," *All Things Considered*, April 9, 2021, https://www.npr.org/2021/04/09/985104612/conspiracy-charges-bring-proud-boys-history-of-violence-into-spotlight.

154. Nicole Disser, "Gavin McInnes and His 'Proud Boys' Want to Make Men Great Again," *Bedford + Bowery*, July 28, 2016, https://web.archive.org/web/20190209020443/https://bedfordandbowery.com/2016/07/gavin-mcinnes-and-his-proud-boys-want-to-make-white-men-great-again.

155. Jay Firestone offers this example from a Proud Boy bar crawl: "John's pristine MAGA hat was adorned with an enamel pin of Pepe the frog—until Sal

walked over, plucked the pin off John's hat, and put it on his own. Sal then walked away, without a word exchanged." Jay Firestone, "Three Months inside Alt-Right New York," *Commune*, Winter 2020, https://communemag .com/alt-right-new-york.

156. Quoted in Southern Poverty Law Center, "Proud Boys." There is a bizarre arrogance to this statement. No one in the Proud Boys could be said to have "creat[ed] the modern world." They just inherited it, like the rest of us. I am reminded of Sakai's observation that "fascism *never* appears in public as its secret parasitic self but always in some other grandiose guise." Mussolini told his followers they were reviving the Roman Empire. The Nazis imagined that they were the return of an ancient race of warriors. The Taliban presented themselves as the true followers of the Prophet. "None of these guises are in the least bit true, of course, but are closer to political fantasy played with real guns for real stakes." J. Sakai, "The Shock of Recognition: Looking at Hamerquist's Fascism and Anti-Fascism," in *Confronting Fascism: Discussion Documents for a Militant Movement* (Montreal: Kersplebedeb, 2017), 116–17.

157. McInnes, "Introducing: The Proud Boys." Laura Jedeed reports: "I personally witnessed a breakfast cereal initiation at a rally with a group of teenage Proud Boys, which consisted of playful punches and a great deal of laughter. However, I also heard a report of a Second Degree initiate who had his ribs cracked during the ordeal." Laura Jedeed, "Making Monsters: Right-Wing Creation of the Liberal Enemy" (B.A. thesis, Reed College, 2019), 76.

158. Reid and Valasik, *Alt-Right Gangs*, 26–27.

159. Southern Poverty Law Center, "Proud Boys."

160. Gavin McInnes, "Some Clarification on the 4th Degree," *Proud Boy Magazine*, https://archive.is/o1ia1#selection-627.0-627.493, accessed June 2021.

161. Jedeed, "Making Monsters," 106, 109. Effie Baum points to this incident as the moment that media coverage shifted and became increasingly critical of the group. Effie Baum, in conversation, August 4, 2021.

162. Gene Johnson, Martha Bellisle, and Michael Balsamo, "Feds: Member of Proud Boys Arrested in Washington State," ABC News, February 3, 2021, https://abcnews.go.com/US/wireStory/feds-member-proud-boys-arrested -washington-state-75668692.

163. Reid and Valasik, *Alt-Right Gangs*, 26.

164. "A victory fable portrays the enemy as cowardly, dishonorable, and ultimately powerless in the face of the noble protagonist. A victim fable portrays the enemy as a threat to innocent bystanders. In order to be successful, groups that strive to create a vision of the enemy must create both types of fables. A propagandistic diet of nothing but victory fables would result in the impression that the enemy is no match for the group. Without a perceived threat, there is no need for an alliance to combat the threat. A

group that constructs nothing but victim fables, on the other hand, runs the risk of looking weak and ineffective." Jedeed, "Making Monsters," 105.

165. Quoted in Burley, "Alt-Right Gangs."

166. He says it was a joke. E. J. Dickson, "The Rise and Fall of the Proud Boys," *Rolling Stone*, June 15, 2021, https://www.rollingstone.com/culture/culture-features/proud-boys-far-right-group-1183966.

167. See Disser, "Gavin McInnes and His 'Proud Boys'." Also relevant here is Jedeed's discussion of "troll tactics." Jedeed, "Making Monsters," 64–66.

168. Julia DeCook, for example, writes: "One key facet of the Proud Boys . . . is how they very much function like a fraternity or[,] more accurately, a gang: their gatherings often involve heavy amounts of drinking and violence, there are rituals involved in gaining status in the group, and there is a uniform and agreed upon logo (including colors) to signify their group identity." DeCook, "Memes and Symbolic Violence," 491. Political Research Associates described the Proud Boys as a "Republican Party Street Gang." Pointing particularly to the violent initiation rituals, they argue, "Although the Proud Boys may present themselves as merely an edgy male drinking club, the organization has the hallmarks of an organized gang." Gorcenski, "The Proud Boys." The Anti-Defamation League likewise asserts, "the Proud Boys bear many of the hallmarks of a gang." Anti-Defamation League, "The Proud Boys."

169. Reid and Valasik, *Alt-Right Gangs*, 24–28, 42, 54–55.

170. Burley, "Alt-Right Gangs."

171. Reid and Valasik, *Alt-Right Gangs*, 24. In September 2020, Fred Perry announced that the company would be discontinuing the black-and-gold design because of its association with Proud Boys. Southern Poverty Law Center, "Proud Boys."

172. Travis and Hardy, *Skinheads*, 23.

173. O'Connor, "Trump's Useful Thugs."

174. O'Connor, "Trump's Useful Thugs." Among those arrested after the Metropolitan Club attack was Irvin Antillon, a member of Battalion 49, who also attended Unite the Right as a member of Fraternal Order of the Alt-Knights. Brett Barrouquere, "Skinhead 'Irv' among Five Charged in Proud Boys' New York Assault," Southern Poverty Law Center, October 22, 2018, https://www.splcenter.org/hatewatch/2018/10/22/skinhead-irv-among-five-charged-proud-boys-new-york-city-assault. For more on the connections between Proud Boys, B49, 211, and other clearly racist organizations, see Hatewatch Staff, "Do You Want Bigots, Gavin? Because This Is How You Get Bigots," August 10, 2017, https://www.splcenter.org/hatewatch/2017/08/10/do-you-want-bigots-gavin-because-how-you-get-bigots.

175. Quoted in Carol Schaeffer, "Inside the Proud Boy Event That Sparked Violence Outside of Uptown GOP Club," *Bedford + Bowery*, October 13, 2018,

https://bedfordandbowery.com/2018/10/inside-the-proud-boy-event-that-sparked-violence-outside-of-uptown-gop-club.

176. Southern Poverty Law Center, "Proud Boys"; Stern, *Proud Boys and the White Ethnostate*, 74; and Reid and Valasik, *Alt-Right Gangs*, 11.

177. Quoted in Southern Poverty Law Center, "Proud Boys."

178. Quoted in Ben Makuch and Mack Lamoureux, "A Proud Boys Lawyer Wanted to Be a Nazi Terrorist," *Vice*, December 8, 2020, https://www.vice.com/en/article/wx8xp4/a-proud-boys-lawyer-wanted-to-be-a-nazi-terrorist. See also Andy Campbell, "Proud Boys' Former Lawyer Used the Gang in an Assassination Plot, Texas Police Say," *HuffPost*, April 15, 2020, https://www.huffpost.com/entry/proud-boys-lawyer-jason-lee-van-dyke_n_5e97a760c5b6a92100e1c6e7; and Greg Land, "Ex-Proud Boys Lawyer Van Dyke Suspended over Threats to Bar Complaint," *Law.com*, February 25, 2019, https://www.law.com/texaslawyer/2019/02/25/ex-proud-boys-lawyer-van-dyke-suspended-over-threats-to-bar-complaint.

179. Southern Poverty Law Center, "Proud Boys."

180. NPR, "The Capitol Siege: The Arrested and Their Stories," *All Things Considered*, July 16, 2021, https://www.npr.org/2021/02/09/965472049/the-capitol-siege-the-arrested-and-their-stories; Dinah Pulver et al., "Capitol Riot Arrests: See Who's Been Charged Across the U.S.," *USA Today*, July 15, 2021, https://eu.usatoday.com/storytelling/capitol-riot-mob-arrests; Clare Hymes, Cassidy McDonald, and Eleanor Watson, "More Than 535 Arrested So Far in Capitol Riot Case, While More Than 300 Suspects Remain Unidentified," CBS News, July 16, 2021, https://www.cbsnews.com/news/capitol-riot-arrests-latest-2021-06-24; Madison Hall et al., "579 People Have Been Charged in The Capitol Insurrection So Far. This Searchable Table Shows Them All," *Business Insider*, July 16, 2021, https://www.insider.com/all-the-us-capitol-pro-trump-riot-arrests-charges-names-2021-1; and Dreisbach, "Conspiracy Charges." Prosecutors allege that as many as sixty Proud Boys were involved in planning the assault. Dickson, "The Rise and Fall of the Proud Boys."

181. Southern Poverty Law Center, "Proud Boys"; and, Alanna Durkin Richer, "Proud Boys Leader Was Government Informant, Records Show," AP News, January 27, 2021, https://apnews.com/article/proud-boys-government-informant-dc84086d78b688bc585f874452d2b481.

182. Aram Roston, "Exclusive: Proud Boys Leader Was 'Prolific' Informer for Law Enforcement," Reuters, January 27, 2021, https://www.reuters.com/article/us-usa-proudboys-leader-exclusive-idUSKBN29W1PE.

183. Quoted in Marissa J. Lang, "As Fractures Emerge among Proud Boys, Experts Warn of a Shift toward Extremist Violence," *Washington Post*, February 26, 2021.

184. Cassie Miller, "Accusations in the Mirror: How the Radical Right

Blames Rising Political Violence on the Left," *Southern Poverty Law Center*, June 11, 2019, https://www.splcenter.org/hatewatch/2019/06/11/accusations-mirror-how-radical-right-blames-rising-political-violence-left.

185. Wilson, "Who Are The Proud Boys."

186. Kelly Weill, "The Disturbing Ties between Philly Cops and Far-Right Proud Boys," *Daily Beast*, July 16, 2020, https://www.thedailybeast.com/the-disturbing-ties-between-philadelphia-police-and-far-right-proud-boys; and Jason Wilson, "FBI Now Classifies Far-Right Proud Boys as Extremist Group, Documents Say," *Guardian*, November 19, 2018.

187. Michael Kunzelman, "Police Officer Retires after Far-Right Group Ties Revealed," ABC News, November 1, 2019, https://abcnews.go.com/us/wirestory/police-officer-retires-group-ties-revealed-66688205.

188. "Plaquemines Parish Sheriff's Office Fires 'Proud Boy' Deputy Brian Green," NOLA.com, August 18, 2018, https://www.nola.com/news/crime_police/article_ba2e2b32-82fa-5e52-b879-57c416613400.html.

189. Katie Shepherd, "ICE Contractor Posted Bail for Proud Boy Jailed in Portland for Assault," *Willamette Week*, May 15, 2019.

190. Tess Owen, "Chicago Police Are Investigating an Officer Accused of Being a Proud Boy," *Vice*, May 26, 2020, vice.com/amp/en/article/v7ged9/chicago-police-are-investigating-an-officer-accused-of-being-a-proud-boy.

191. Weill, "The Disturbing Ties between Philly Cops."

192. Christopher Mathias, "A National Guardsman Sent to LA Protests Is under Investigation for Ties to Proud Boys," *HuffPost*, July 7, 2020, https://www.huffpost.com/entry/national-guard-proud-boys-california-black-lives-matter_n_5efe44a5c5b612083c592f32.

193. Tarrio told a reporter, "Portland is the epicenter for all the issues we're having across the country." Quoted in Audrey McNamara, "Hundreds Gather in Portland for Dueling Rallies between Proud Boys and Counter Demonstrators," CBS News, September 26, 2020, https://www.cbsnews.com/news/portland-prepares-for-large-right-wing-rally-in-support-of-president-trump.

194. Katie Shepherd, "Texts between Portland Police and Patriot Prayer Ringleader Joey Gibson Show Warm Exchange," *Willamette Week*, February 14, 2019; and Jason Wilson, "Exclusive: Video Shows Portland Officers Made Deal with Far-Right Group Leader," *Guardian*, March 1, 2019.

195. Vysotsky, *American Antifa*, 159; Christopher Mathias and Andy Campbell, "Violent Proto-Fascists Came to Portland. The Police Went after the Anti-Fascists," *HuffPost*, August 5, 2018, https://www.huffpost.com/entry/portland-patriot-prayer-proud-boys-police-antifascists_n_5b668b7de4b0de86f4a22faf; Jason Wilson, "Portland Far-Right Rally: Police Charge Counterprotesters with Batons Drawn," *Guardian*, August 5, 2018; Arun Gupta, "Riotlandia: Why Portland Has Become the Epicenter of Far-Right Violence," *The Intercept*, August 16, 2019, https://theintercept.com/2019/08/16/portland-far-right-rally;

and Suzette Smith, "Portland Police Stand by as Armed Alt-Right Protesters and Antifascists Brawl," *Portland Mercury*, August 23, 2020.

Mike German, a former FBI agent who infiltrated white supremacist organizations, describes the larger pattern: "Law enforcement treated violent far-right militant groups at public protests differently than it treated nonviolent anti-racism protesters. The Proud Boys fit in that milieu. . . . They would commit violence with law enforcement standing by, and in many cases, [police] appeared to be enabling far-right militant groups to come into their communities to commit violence. Then they'd allow them to leave." Quoted in Dickson, "The Rise and Fall of the Proud Boys."

196. Quoted in Katie Shepherd, "Portland Police Saw Right-Wing Protesters as 'Much More Mainstream' Than Leftist Ones," *Willamette Week*, June 27, 2018. This bias is long-standing. In his 1994 book *Skinhead Street Gangs*, Portland Police Bureau gang detective Loren Christensen advises the cops, when preparing for white supremacist demonstrations, "Gather intelligence in the left-wing community. . . . counterdemonstrators are frequently the instigators." Christensen, *Skinhead Street Gangs*, 214.

197. Reid and Valasik, *Alt-Right Gangs*, 32.

198. Jo Ann Hardesty, "Statement from Commissioner Jo Ann Hardesty regarding PPB Texts with Patriot Prayer Leader," news release, February 14, 2019, City of Portland, https://www.portlandoregon.gov/hardesty/article/712673.

199. Quoted in Associated Press, "FBI Enlisted Proud Boys Leader to Inform on Antifa, Lawyer Says," oregonlive.com, March 30, 2021, https://www.oregonlive.com/nation/2021/03/fbi-enlisted-proud-boys-leader-to-inform-on-antifa-lawyer-says.html.

200. O'Connor, "Trump's Useful Thugs."

201. Quoted in Firestone, "Three Months inside Alt-Right New York."

202. Pawl BaZile, "The Kids Are Alt-Knight," officialproudboys.com, [n.d.], https://web.archive.org/web/20170425192820/http:/officialproudboys.com/news/the-kids-are-alt-knights, accessed June 2021.

203. Quoted in Jason Wilson, "The Decline of the Proud Boys: What Does the Future Hold for Far-Right Group?," *Guardian*, February 13, 2021.

204. Quoted in Lang, "As Fractures Emerge among Proud Boys."

205. Will Carless, "Proud Boys Splintering after Capitol Riot, Revelations about Leader. Will More Radical Factions Emerge?" *USA Today*, February 12, 2021.

206. Southern Poverty Law Center, "Brien James," [n.d.], https://www.splcenter.org/fighting-hate/extremist-files/individual/brien-james, accessed June 2021.

207. Quoted in Hatewatch Staff, "Do You Want Bigots, Gavin?"

208. Will Sommer, "New Proud Boy Rules: Less Fighting, Less Wanking," *Daily Beast*, November 27, 2018, https://www.thedailybeast.com/new-proud-boy-rules-less-fighting-less-wanking.

209. Quoted in Claire Goforth, "Far-Right Conflict following Trump Loss Spills onto the Internet," *Daily Dot*, November 11, 2020, https://www.dailydot .com/debug/far-right-infighting-trump-defeat.

210. Tom Porter, "The Proud Boys Are Using Trump's 'Stand By' Remark as a Recruiting Tool, Rebranding to Incorporate What They See as His Call to Action," *Business Insider*, September 30, 2020, https://www.businessinsider .com/proud-boys-are-use-trump-remark-to-rebrand-recruit-2020-9.

211. Quoted in Kelly Weill, "The Post-Election Proud Boys Meltdown Is Here, and It's Ugly," *Daily Beast*, November 11, 2020, https://www.thedailybeast .com/the-post-election-proud-boys-meltdown-is-here-and-its-ugly.

212. Estaban Parra and Brittany Horn, "Delaware US Senate Candidate Thanks Proud Boys for Providing Free Security at Rally," *Delaware Online*, October 10, 2020, https://www.delawareonline.com/story/news/2020/10/01/witzke -thanks-proud-boys-providing-free-security-rally/5878156002.

213. Rebekah Castor, "'Proud Boys' Provide Security at Pro-America Rally in Milton," WEAR-TV.com, October 23, 2020, https://weartv.com/news/local/ proud-boys-provide-security-at-pro-america-rally-in-milton.

214. Kelly Weill, "How the Proud Boys Became Roger Stone's Private Army," *Daily Beast*, January 29, 2019, https://www.thedailybeast.com/how -the-proud-boys-became-roger-stones-personal-army-6.

215. Troy Brynelson and Sergio Olmos, "Far Right Protest Brawler Assists with Security at Clark County GOP Meeting," opb.org (Oregon Public Broadcasting), February 24, 2021, https://www.opb.org/article/2021/02/25/ clark-county-republicans-tusitala-tiny-toese.

216. Quoted in Michelle L. Price, "GOP Officials in Nevada Seek Probe of Proud Boys Ties to Censure Vote," *Las Vegas Sun*, May 24, 2021.

217. Quoted in David Siders, "'It's Insane': Proud Boys Furor Tests Limits of Trump's GOP," *Politico*, May 27, 2021, https://www.politico.com/ news/2021/05/27/nevada-gop-proud-boys-491138.

218. Price, "GOP Officials in Nevada Seek Probe"; Siders, "It's Insane"; and Rory Appleton, "Activists with Ties to Proud Boys May Seek Leadership of Clark County GOP," *Las Vegas Review-Journal*, May 21, 2021.

219. Quoted in Tess Riski, "Multnomah County Republican Party Plans Recall Vote of Chairman Who Advocated for Diversity," *Willamette Week*, May 4, 2021.

220. Matt Shuham, "'You Are Full of Poop': A Proud Boy-Fueled Power Struggle Divides Portland-Area GOP," *Talking Points Memo*, June 4, 2021, https:// talkingpointsmemo.com/news/you-are-full-of-poop-a-proud-boy-fueled- power-struggle-divides-portland-area-gop.

221. Quoted in Sophie Peel, "Multnomah County Republican Party Signed Agreement with Proud Boy-Affiliated Security Team at Portland Meeting," *Willamette Week*, May 10, 2021.

222. Sophie Peel, "The Multnomah County Republican Party Splintered Monday

Night," *Willamette Week*, May 19, 2021; and, Shuham, "You Are Full of Poop."

223. Gavin McInnes holds Canadian and British citizenship but lives in the United States as a permanent resident. Simon Houpt, "Everything inside Gavin McInnes," *Globe and Mail*, August 18, 2017. For a look at the attitudes of some of the people of color involved in the Alt-Right, see Arun Gupta, "Why Young Men of Color Are Joining White Supremacist Groups," *Daily Beast*, September 6, 2018, https://www.thedailybeast.com/why-young-men-of-color-are-joining-white-supremacist-groups.

224. Christian Picciolini, a reformed nazi skinhead, told NPR that Western chauvinism "translates to 'European chauvinism' or 'European pride,' which would have been the same thing as 'white pride.'... Proud Boys are probably the closest thing to what I was 30 years ago, and I was a white power skinhead." Quoted in Dreisbach, "Conspiracy Charges."

225. "Fascism may be defined as a form of political behavior marked by obsessive preoccupation with community decline, humiliation, or victimhood and by compensatory cults of unity, energy, and purity, in which a mass-based party of committed nationalist militants, working in uneasy but effective collaboration with traditional elites, abandons democratic liberties and pursues with redemptive violence and without ethical or legal restraints goals of internal cleansing and externals expansion." Robert O. Paxton, *The Anatomy of Fascism* (New York: Vintage Books, 2005), 218.

226. Stern, *Proud Boys and the White Ethnostate*, 74.

227. Stern, 125.

228. "Friendship, tutelage, and religious fellowship provided the microinteractional norms—the rules behind the rules—that enabled people to make decisions without constant negotiation over the terms of engagement. The problem ... was that, along with caring, cooperation, and a complex equality that made for mutual learning, those relationships also came with norms that undermined democratic projects: variously, exclusivity, deference, conflict avoidance, and an antipathy to the rules that might have made for more accountability." Polletta, *Freedom Is an Endless Meeting*, 222.

229. "[Crises] occurred at pressure points in the associational relationships on which participatory democracy was based, chiefly friendship, tutelage, and religious fellowship. Where friendship's natural exclusivity came up against the demands of expanding the group, where organizers' commitment to respecting residents' own political learning process came up against the need to define political aims, and where religious fellows' commitment to cooperation came up against the absolutism of personal conscience—at these points conflicts occurred." Polletta, 217.

230. Perhaps not entirely benign: "Football [soccer], and especially the violence articulated around it, also provided one arena for the expression of the

skinhead's concern with a particular, collective, masculine self-conception, involving an identification of masculinity with physical toughness, and an unwillingness to back down in the face of 'trouble.' The violence also involved the mobs' stress on collective solidarity and mutual support in times of 'need.'" Clarke, "The Skinheads and the Magical Recovery of Community," 119. Bray, *Antifa*, 121–25, considers soccer's place in contemporary antifascist culture in some detail; and Vysotsky, *American Antifa*, 149, describes efforts to push fascists out of soccer crowds. On tattoos, Vysotsky also notes that they "served as a means of bonding among antifascist activists." Vysotsky, *American Antifa*, 113.

231. Vysotsky, *American Antifa*, 120. In the summer of 2019, one wall of a vacant building not far from my home in Portland bore a massive piece of graffiti that declared with startling directness, "Rose City Bovver Boys: Nazi Killers."

232. Quoted in "Bonus Episode One: The Minneapolis Baldies and Anti-Racist Action Transcript Part Two," *It Did Happen Here*, podcast transcript, March 11, 2021, http://itdidhappenherepodcast.com/transcripts/bonus_1_transcript .html.

233. Security requirements: Burley, *Fascism Today*, 255–56.

234. Vysotsky, *American Antifa*, 91.

235. Vysotsky, 97.

236. Vysotsky, 72.

237. Burley, *Fascism Today*, 255.

238. See Don Hamerquist, "Fascism and Anti-Fascism," in *Confronting Fascism: Discussion Documents for a Militant Movement* (Montreal: Kersplebedeb, 2017), 72–73.

239. Bray, *Antifa*, 193.

240. Quoted in Bray, 193.

241. "Episode Eight: SHARPer Times."

242. For a depiction of this dynamic in a Montreal SHARP crew, see Ferguson, "Taking It Back, Making It Strong!," 47–48.

243. Quoted in Vysotsky, *American Antifa*, 103. At least, to the best of my knowledge, none of the antiracist or antifascist groups I've discussed here further complicated matters by engaging in illegal activities for commercial reasons. As I discussed in the preceding essay, a reliance on the black market represents a serious obstacle in a gang's efforts to act as a force for social change. (Thanks to Peter Little for pointing this out to me in conversation, July 14, 2021.)

244. Don Hamerquist cautions, "A revolutionary culture must not incorporate violence into its internal functioning . . . [but] this [restraint] is not at all easy to combine with the importance of militance in the general struggle, with the necessity to reject strategic pacifism, and with the need to sharply

challenge and vigorously debate various ideas and attitudes which inevitably will be a part of the scene." Hamerquist, "Fascism and Anti-Fascism," 85. Regarding reputational costs, Mike German points to the devastating effect a fatal bar fight had on the IRA's support in the community. Mike German, *Thinking Like a Terrorist: Insights of a Former FBI Undercover Agent* (Washington, DC: Potomac Books, 2007), 170.

245. The canonical text on the connection between patriarchal culture and police infiltration is Courtney Desiree Morris, "Why Misogynists Make Great Informants: How Gender Violence on the Left Enables State Violence in Radical Communities," *make/shift*, Spring/Summer 2010.

246. Effie Baum helped me to connect these dots, in conversation, August 4, 2021.

247. Hamerquist, "Fascism and Anti-Fascism," 57.

248. Quoted in Bray, *Antifa*, 191.

249. Bray, 191.

250. "Bonus Episode One: The Minneapolis Baldies."

251. "How the Midwest Was Won"; and Vysotsky, *American Antifa*, 52–53.

252. "Combating serious fascist tendencies though physical and military confrontations is no joke. It requires a serious attitude towards internal security often involving the limitation of discussion and debate and the compartmentalization of information according to 'need to know' criteria. It requires a conscious decision to avoid those confrontations that might end in defeat or use up too much of our scant military resources . . . organizationally, there is an inevitable pressure here towards clandestinity. Strategically, the direction is towards military considerations taking priority over political ones. Under such circumstances the most dedicated organizers will often be forced to stand aside from potentials for mass militancy in order to maintain and protect a military potential." Hamerquist, "Fascism and Anti-Fascism," 72–73.

253. Polletta writes of the crises troubling the various movements she studied: "What made these conflicts so hard to overcome was that, to do so, the activists involved in them would have had to go outside the normative framework that governed their interactions." Polletta, *Freedom Is an Endless Meeting*, 217–18.

254. Vysotsky, *American Antifa*, 172.

255. Vysotsky, 146. Another social scientist likewise described the role of SHARP in the Montreal skinhead scene in terms of "policing." Ferguson, "'Taking It Back, Making It Strong!'," 40–43.

256. Vysotsky, *American Antifa*, 147.

257. Vysotsky, 158.

258. Vysotsky, 156.

259. Vysotsky, 156.

260. Additional political and security problems arise when a semi-clandestine

group feels ownership over an issue and expects deference from the broader left. The insistence on anonymity greatly undercuts any potential for legitimacy, partly because others in the movement (not to mention the public at large) may not know who it is that is tagging people as enemies, calling for boycotts and ostracism, and sometimes engaging in intimidation and violence.

261. For a discussion of the problems, see "Community Self-Defense with the John Brown Gun Club," *It Could Happen Here*, October 21, 2021, https://www.iheart.com/podcast/1119-it-could-happen-here-30717896/episode/community-self-defense-with-the-john-brown-88299224.

262. If we, following Vysotsky, view Antifa as an alternative system of justice, it may be worth considering the criteria for legitimacy that Harry Mika and Kieran McEvoy developed in the context of alternative justice projects in Northern Ireland: (1) *mandate* (is there a demonstrated need?); (2) *moral authority* (has the community appointed the organization to act on its behalf?); (3) *partnership* (does the organization make use of the skills and resources of the community and address its needs?); (4) *competence* (does the organization have the requisite skills to meet its objectives?); (5) *practice* (does the program respect established standards of justice and respond to community concerns?); (6) *transparency* (are there "mechanisms for public scrutiny, local management and control, and opportunities for public input"?); and, (7) *accountability* (is the program evaluated according to its stated standards, community impact, and overall effectiveness?). Harry Mika and Kieran McEvoy, "Restorative Justice in Conflict: Paramilitarism, Community, and the Construction of Legitimacy in Northern Ireland," *Comparative Justice Review* 4, nos. 3–4 (2001): 307–10.

263. It must be said that, thus far, principle has done a remarkable job. One report "funded in part by the UK security and intelligence agencies," examining both the British and the American antifascist movements, concludes: "While the willingness to use confrontational violence separates militant anti-fascism from non-militant forms, militant anti-fascists exercise restraint in their use of violence. This is significant. It clearly challenges simplistic associations with terrorism and the planning of terrorist acts and/or mass violence that threatens life. The claim that fascism is defined by an ultra-violent credo imposes a value-based, prefigurative boundary on militant anti-fascists in both their use and rhetorical representation of violence. Strategic concerns factor too, such as the risk that violent escalation will lead either to group isolation from the wider anti-fascist coalition or dissolution as a result of increasing state repression. Internal cultures of decision-making and recruitment structures function as further dynamics of restraint." Copsey and Merrill, *Understanding 21st-Century Militant Anti-Fascism*, 2, 4.

264. For a surprisingly useful discussion of antifascist strategies for legitimating violence, and the degree to which they rely precisely on its relative restraint and infrequency, see Copsey, *Understanding 21st-Century Militant Anti-Fascism*, 32–33.

265. M. Treloar, in conversation, circa 2011.

266. Quoted in "How the Midwest Was Won."

Postscript: Neither Gangs nor Governments

1. The personal costs are significant and should also be taken into account. Peter Little considers his own firsthand experience with skinhead politics: "It's a long list of folks who brought me up, or who came up with me, who are now dead. Addiction and trauma—they are pretty significant as the reasons for that. And I can certainly say that a lot of that trauma, addiction, and violence as well, certainly emerged as a consequence of the militarization or the prioritization of violence as methodology." "Episode Eight: SHARPer Times," *It Did Happen Here*, podcast transcript, http://itdidhappenherepod cast.com/transcripts/episode8_transcript.html.

2. J. Sakai argues that while criminal gangs are not in themselves inherently fascist, "they can resonate along that line": "[T]here are fascist precursors in the mass gang subculture. A mass armed criminal organization of declassed men that wants not only to have a rough control of the local population but have a linked economic and political program of domination has already taken a step toward fascism." J. Sakai, "The Shock of Recognition: Looking at Hamerquist's Fascism and Anti-fascism," in *Confronting Fascism: Discussion Documents for a Militant Movement* (Montreal: Kersplebedeb, 2017), 179, 181.

3. For an account of the split in the First International, see Robert Graham, *We Do Not Fear Anarchy, We Invoke It: The First International and the Origins of the Anarchist Movement* (Oakland: AK Press, 2015).

4. Quoted in Iain McIntyre, "A Conversation with Black Mask," in *Realizing the Impossible: Art Against Authority*, eds. Josh MacPhee and Erik Reuland (Oakland: AK Press, 2007), 161.

5. Fray Baroque and Tegan Eanelli, eds., *Queer Ultraviolence: Abridged Bash Back Anthology* (n.p.: Little Black Cart, 2013), cover art.

6. The Invisible Committee, *The Coming Insurrection* ([no publication information listed]), 78. As usual there is an element of idealization in all of this, even if it is the idealism of negation. The Invisible Committee comes close to admitting as much, positing the gang as a kind of fantasy being, albeit one born of a bourgeois nightmare: "These gangs who flee work, who adopt the names of their neighborhoods, and confront the police are the nightmare of

the good, individualized French citizen: they embody everything he has renounced, all the possible joy he will never experience." Invisible Committee, *Coming Insurrection*, 24.

7. scott crow, "Liberatory Community Armed Self-Defense: Approaches toward a Theory," in *Setting Sights: Histories and Reflections on Community Armed Self-Defense* (Oakland: PM Press, 2018), 8. On ARA's influence on his thinking, and on his decision to take up arms after Katrina, see scott crow, "On Violence, Disasters, Defense, and Transformation: Setting Sights for the Future," in *Setting Sights: Histories and Reflections on Community Armed Self-Defense* (Oakland: PM Press, 2018), 219–21.

8. crow, "Liberatory Community Armed Self-Defense," 10–11.

9. crow, 11.

10. crow, 11–12.

11. Quotes in this paragraph and the one following are drawn from an interview with scott crow conducted by the author, November 18 and 19, 2021.

Index

"Passim" (literally "scattered") indicates intermittent discussion of a topic over a cluster of pages.

Also by Kristian Williams

Resist Everything Except Temptation:
The Anarchist Philosophy of Oscar Wilde
(AK Press, 2020)

Whither Anarchism?
(AK Press, 2018)

Between the Bullet and the Lie:
Essays on Orwell
(AK Press, 2017)

Our Enemies in Blue:
Police and Power in America, 3rd ed.
(AK Press, 2015)

Fire the Cops:
Essays, Lectures, and Journalism
(Kersplebedeb, 2014)

Hurt:
Notes on Torture in a Modern Democracy
(Microcosm, 2012)

American Methods:
Torture and the Logic of Domination
(South End Press, 2006)

AK PRESS is small, in terms of staff and resources, but we also manage to be one of the world's most productive anarchist publishing houses. We publish close to twenty books every year, and distribute thousands of other titles published by like-minded independent presses and projects from around the globe. We're entirely worker run and democratically managed. We operate without a corporate structure—no boss, no managers, no bullshit.

The **FRIENDS OF AK PRESS** program is a way you can directly contribute to the continued existence of AK Press, and ensure that we're able to keep publishing books like this one! Friends pay $25 a month directly into our publishing account ($30 for Canada, $35 for international), and receive a copy of every book AK Press publishes for the duration of their membership! Friends also receive a discount on anything they order from our website or buy at a table: 50% on AK titles, and 30% on everything else. We have a Friends of AK ebook program as well: $15 a month gets you an electronic copy of every book we publish for the duration of your membership. *You can even sponsor a very discounted membership for someone in prison.*

Email **friendsofak@akpress.org** for more info, or visit the website: **https://www.akpress.org/friends.html**.

There are always great book projects in the works—so sign up now to become a Friend of AK Press, and let the presses roll!